MEDIA, FEMINISM, CULTURAL STUDIES

Stepping Forward: Essays, Lectures and Interviews
by Wolfgang Iser

Wild Zones: Pornography, Art and Feminism
by Kelly Ives

Global Media Warning: Explorations of Radio, Television and the Press
by Oliver Whitehorne

'Cosmo Woman': The World of Women's Magazines
by Oliver Whitehorne

Andrea Dworkin
by Jeremy Mark Robinson

Cixous, Irigaray, Kristeva: The Jouissance of French Feminism
by Kelly Ives

Sex in Art: Pornography and Pleasure in Painting and Sculpture
by Cassidy Hughes

The Erotic Object: Sexuality in Sculpture
From Prehistory to the Present Day
by Susan Quinnell

Women in Pop Music
by Helen Challis

Detonation Britain: Nuclear War in the UK
by Jeremy Mark Robinson

Julia Kristeva: Art, Love, Melancholy, Philosophy, Semiotics
by Kelly Ives

Luce Irigaray: Lips, Kissing, and the Politics of Sexual Difference
by Kelly Ives

Helene Cixous I Love You: The Jouissance of Writing
by Kelly Ives

The Poetry of Cinema
by John Madden

The Sacred Cinema of Andrei Tarkovsky
by Jeremy Mark Robinson

Disney Business, Disney Films, Disney Lands
Daniel Cerruti

Feminism and Shakespeare
by B.D. Barnacle

SEXING HARDY

Thomas Hardy and Feminism

SEXING HARDY

Thomas Hardy and Feminism

Margaret Elvy

CRESCENT MOON

CRESCENT MOON PUBLISHING
P.O. Box 393
Maidstone
Kent, ME14 5XU
United Kingdom

First published 1998. Second edition 2007.
© Margaret Elvy 1998, 2007.

Printed and bound in Great Britain.
Set in Book Antiqua 9 on 14pt and Gill Sans display.
Designed by Radiance Graphics.

British Library Cataloguing in Publication data

Elvy, Margaret
Sexing Hardy: Thomas Hardy and Feminism
1. Hardy, Thomas, 1840-1928 – Criticism and interpretation
2. English fiction – 19th century – History and criticism
3. Feminism in literature
I. Title

823.8

ISBN 1-86171-065-8
ISBN-13 978-1-86171-065-9

Contents

ABBREVIATIONS

J	*Jude the Obscure*
T	*Tess of the D'Urbervilles*
R	*The Return of the Native*
W	*The Woodlanders*
M	*The Mayor of Casterbridge*
F	*Far From the Madding Crowd*
U	*Under the Greenwood Tree*
PBE	*A Pair of Blue Eyes*
WB	*The Well-Beloved*
TT	*Two on a Tower*
Lao	*A Laocidean*
DR	*Desperate Remedies*
HE	*The Hand of Ethelberta*
TM	*The Trumpet-Major*
D	*The Dynasts*
CP	*Complete Poems*
Love	*Hardy's Love Poems*
SS	*The Short Stories of Thomas Hardy*
Lit	*The Literary Notebooks of Thomas Hardy*
Let	*The Collected Letters of Thomas Hardy*
Per	*The Personal Notebooks of Thomas Hardy*
L	*The Life and Work of Thomas Hardy*
PW	*Personal Writings*
H	*The Sense of Sex*, ed. Margaret Higonnet

SEXING HARDY

Thomas Hardy and Feminism

PART ONE
Thomas Hardy

Thomas Hardy (courtesy of Dorset County Museum)

An illustration from the serialization of *The Mayor of Casterbridge*

I

Introduction:
Thomas Hardy Criticism

A mass of critical data has grown up around Thomas Hardy. He is one of the most discussed authors in the language. This sample from critic John Peck is typical of the kind of Hardy criticism which sees in his work a marvellous evocation of hidden emotions, often vaguely called the unconscious:

> Hardy offers us something more exciting than a mirror image of life... he always writes with a sense of a force which is elusive and cannot be explained... his most extraordinary ability is to create and convey a sense of a natural energy at work in life. (J. Peck, 59)

One could also cite Thomas Hardy critics such as Ian Gregor, John Bayley, Michael Millgate, Merryn Williams, Jean Brooks, Arnold Kettle, Irving Howe, David Cecil, Philip Larkin, W.H. Auden and a host of others as producing similar criticism. Hardy has had it easy, as far as most criticism is concerned. The collections of essays and criticism (such as those edited by Albert Guerard, Anne Smith, Lance St John Butler, Dale

Kramer, Harold Bloom, Norman Page, R.P. Draper and Phillip Mallett, the stalwarts of any public or college library) were sincere efforts, but hardly ever offered something other than humanist, formal, and often vague criticism. Even in the 1980s and 1990s books on Thomas Hardy kept coming out which preferred not to acknowledge writers such as Jacques Derrida, Gilles Deleuze, Felix Guattari, Paul de Man, Jean Baudrillard, Mikhail Bakhtin, Jacques Lacan, Annette Kuhn, Laura Mulvey or feminist thinkers such as Julia Kristeva, Luce Irigaray, Gayatri Chakravorty Spivak, Linda Williams, Monique Wittig, Adrienne Rich, Alice Jardine, bell hooks, Judith Butler, Teresa de Lauretis and Elizabeth Grosz.

The two most perceptive collections of essays on the work of Thomas Hardy up to the mid-1990s were edited by Lance St John Butler (1989) and Margaret Higonnet (1993). After Derrida and deconstruction, to take one kind of post-1960s criticism, texts were no longer 'whole', but were, in the words of an important Hardy critic (J. Hillis Miller), 'undecidable'. Texts were 'self-subverting', in the process of dismantling themselves, leading to a multiplicity of sometimes conflicting readings.[1] As a mid-1990s book of feminist criticism said, a heterogeneity of theoretical positions seems to be inevitable (S. Mills, 1994, 283).

Where critics have a field day demolishing Thomas Hardy's art is in his literary style in his fiction. Hardy's style at its worst is marked by 'verbosity and redundance, with ponderous words, clumsily polysyllabic, and unhappy phrases' (I. Baker, 95). Hardy's deliberate complexity or learned allusions do sometimes make his fiction very creaky and ugly. Occasionally, he *is* really bad, so the reader cringes. Often the failures in style occur in lulls between events, for when some dramatic event is taking place, such as the storm over the ricks in *Far From the Madding Crowd*, Hardy's narration is tremendous (but then, only a terrible writer couldn't make a storm work in writing).

Many of the books on Thomas Hardy's fiction stay safe and discuss his Wessex, or his nature poetry, the 'Thomas Hardy' of a rural, nostalgic and now lost world (Denys Kay-Robinson, Hermann Lea, Merryn Williams, W. Sherren, W.J. Keith, John Alcorn, B.A.C. Windle). In this view, 'Hardy' is the 'tragic novelist of character struggling heroically with nature, Fate,

16

or other, pre-eminently non-social forces' (P. Widdowson, 1983, 13). This is the 'Thomas Hardy' the tourist and TV industries promulgate, the 'Thomas Hardy' of expensive television adaptions and tourist board brochures. Hélène Cixous writes that 'the mystery is that we confuse invent and believe.'[2] This is worth keeping in mind, especially with regard to Hardy's characters, who seem so 'real', so that Hardy fans, visiting modern day Marnhull in North Dorset, think they are beholding Tess's 'real' cottage.

Much of Thomas Hardy criticism is of the humanist, formal, New Criticism ilk, taking Hardy's texts as the products of one person (Irving Howe, J.I.M. Stewart, David Cecil, John Bayley, Lascelles Abercrombie, Virginia Woolf, Denys Kay-Robinson, Jean Brooks, Michael Millgate, F.B. Pinion, A. Alvarez, Simon Gatrell, R.P. Draper, Robert Schweik, J.W. Beach, Edmund Blunden, Donald Davie, Merryn Williams, Ian Gregor and Albert Guerard). These were the critics that helped put Hardy into the centre of English literature. Few critics had anything new to say about Hardy's fiction that had not already been said by the 1950s.

Thomas Hardy has had one or two critics that have produced startling work, the most obvious is perhaps D.H. Lawrence, whose *A Study of Thomas Hardy* has provoked much critical debate. Indeed, there is a section of Hardy (meta)criticism devoted to Lawrence on Hardy.

It was surprising, perhaps, that F.R. Leavis left Thomas Hardy out of his Great Tradition. It is odd that Leavis exalted George Eliot and D.H. Lawrence, but not Thomas Hardy. Leavis grudgingly acknowledged the greatness of a dozen of Hardy's poems, but his novels were vastly overrated, Leavis reckoned (Thomas Hardy! Over-rated! As if!).[3] Hardy's work, though, had far too many other critics championing it to be much affected by Leavis's omission.

Another 'Thomas Hardy' beloved of critics is the philosopher, pessimist and sometime Buddhist (authors such as H. Garwood, H.B. Grimditch, Lance St John Butler, P. Braybrooke, Ralph W.W. Elliott, F.R. Southerington, E.J. Brennecke, G.W. Sherman and Jagdish Chandra Dave have written of Hardy's 'philosophy'). This is the 'Thomas Hardy' that became an Existentialist in the 1950s, an inheritor of the German philosophy of Schopenhauer and Nietzsche, a dramatist in the Theatre of the Absurd of Eugene Ionesco, Antonin Artaud and Samuel Beckett.

Thomas Hardy's biographers have not greatly altered his critical status, whether the biographies have been 'sympathetic' (Michael Millgate, Timothy O'Sullivan, Carl J. Weber, R.L. Purdy, F.B. Pinion, F. Halliday), or seen as potentially damaging (Martin Seymour-Smith, Robert Gittings). There have been too few critical views of Hardy's works that use materialism, Marxism, deconstructionism, psychoanalysis, feminism or postmodernism. Critics who have employed some of the more recent critical approaches, loosely termed 'cultural theory', include J. Hillis Miller, Lance St John Butler, John Goode, Roger Ebbatson, J.-J. Lecercle, R. Saldivar, Terry Eagleton, Peter Widdowson, Janie Sénéchal-Teissedou, Charles Lock, Tony Tanner and George Wootton. Critics I would cite as particularly enriching, not including the feminist critics (see below), include Widdowson, Lecercle, Lawrence and Goode, and to a lesser extent, Ebbatson, Tanner and Eagleton.

One might suppose that Tom Hardy's work has been particularly well-served by feminist criticism – there seems to have been a lot of it (Penny Boumelha, Virginia Woolf, Patricia Stubbs, Katherine Rogers, Elaine Showalter, Rosalind Miles, Rosemarie Morgan, Rosemary Sumner, Patricia Ingham, T.R. Wright, Mary Jacobus, Kate Millett, Linda Williams and Marjorie Garson). 'Probably no male author in English literature has been the subject of so much feminist appraisal' wrote Charles Lock (1992, 126). I would disagree: D.H. Lawrence has had just as much attention from feminists, and feminist criticism of Lawrence has generally been of a higher quality. Ditto with Shakespeare.

Feminist critics have been interested by the feminism-in-the-making in Hardy's fiction, and by his female characters.[4] Hardy says a lot about the human, and feminine predicament. His texts manage, through an impressionist approach, to make people 'enlarged and dignified', as Virginia Woolf put it. Hardy's ability to dignify and elevate people is partly what makes him 'the greatest tragic writer among English novelists' (1932, 253f). Much of Hardy criticism is masculinist and sexist, like most literary criticism from the ancient Greeks onwards. However, except in a few cases (Mary Jacobus, Kaja Silverman, Kathleen Blake, Elisabeth Bronfen, Dianne Fallon Sadoff, Linda Williams and Rosemarie

18

Morgan), most feminist Hardy criticism is usually of the well-trodden second wave feminist type, as epitomized by Kate Millet's *Sexual Politics*. Laudable as the attempts of most feminist critics are, their insights into Hardy's work remain limited and disappointing (Rosemary Sumner, Rosalind Miles, Elaine Showalter, Penny Boumelha, Patricia Stubbs, Katherine Rogers and Patricia Ingham). Far and away the best collection of feminist approaches to Hardy's work, and one of the very best books on Hardy, is *The Sense of Sex*, (ed. Margaret Higonnet, 1993).

Thomas Hardy divided up his novels into three groups, and Hardy critics have kept, by and large, to these divisions ever since. The six 'great' / 'tragic' Hardy novels are *Tess of the d'Urbervilles, Jude the Obscure, The Return of the Native, The Mayor of Casterbridge, Far From the Madding Crowd* and *The Woodlanders*. This is the central group of novels that is discussed in nearly every book on Hardy. It corresponds to Hardy's 'Novels of Character and Environment'. Hardy criticism next groups together the 'minor' or 'secondary' novels, which come from the category 'Romances and Fantasies': *Two On a Tower, A Pair of Blue Eyes, The Trumpet-Major, The Well-Beloved* and *Under the Greenwood Tree* (this latter is in Hardy's first group, though hardly any Hardy critic puts it beside *Tess* or *Jude*). This middle group of 'lesser' novels is usually discussed in Hardy criticism, often dealt with in one chapter, with the major novels having a chapter each. The short stories are usually analyzed in the 'minor works' chapter: *Life's Little Ironies, Wessex Tales* and *A Group of Noble Dames*. Then come the novels which are rarely discussed anywhere: *The Hand of Ethelberta, Desperate Remedies* and *A Laodicean*. It is assumed (wrongly, perhaps) that the 'lesser' novels, such as *A Laodicean* and *Desperate Remedies*, have too many faults to make them 'great' or worthy of discussion.

II

Thomas Hardy and Feminism

What are my books but one long plea against 'man's inhumanity to man' – to woman – and to the lower animals? Whatever may be the inherent good or evil of life, it is certain that men make it much worse than it need be.

Thomas Hardy, 1904 (in F. Pinion, 1968, 178)

Is Thomas Hardy a feminist? Are Thomas Hardy's works feminist? How much do his works reflect and bolster the patriarchal attitudes and values of his era, and how much do they question them? What is the relation between Hardy and the feminists of his time? And what is the relation between Hardy's works and the feminism of the early 21st century? These are inter-related questions. We are concerned here with Thomas Hardy's novels, not the man or author himself, and the fiction's relations with contemporary feminism. When we write Hardy we mean the 'Hardy' that is written into the novels, the 'Hardy' who is and is not the narrator of the novels.[1] We mean the 'Hardy' created by the texts, not the biographical, 'real' 'Hardy' who lived at Max Gate in Dorchester, who had certain literary and wealthy friends, who went up to London for 'the season', who bicycled around Dorset, who was fond of pet dogs (the Hardy evoked in the *Life*). Instead of there being a direct connection between

21

author and reader, which humanist criticism assumes, there can be seen at least six levels of mediation: real author > implied author > narrator > narratee > implied reader > real reader.[2] The 'real reader' is thus at a critical distance from the 'real author', 'Thomas Hardy'.

Thomas Hardy's theme is 'Wessexuality', 'Wes-sex-mania', Wessexual politics. Thomas Hardy's works are sexist, patriarchal and masculinist, and yet they question notions of sexism, gender, identity, subjectivity, patriarchy and masculinism.[3] A text such as *Tess of the d'Urbervilles* is 'traditional', and follows patriarchal codes and morals. Yet it also questions them, and offers a number of feminist critiques of late 19th century society. In his letters Hardy proposed feminist views; he wrote to feminists such as the suffragette leader Millicent Fawcett that a child was the mother's own business, not the father's (*Collected Letters*, 3, 238). One can see these feminist sentiments in, for example, Hardy's treatment of Tess in her motherhood: she works in the fields just a few weeks after the birth, even though she is melancholy (she seems to be suffering a mild form of post-natal depression). Tess further subverts patriarchy by taking her child's baptism into her own hands. She goes against her father, the vicar, and the whole church with her self-made baptism.

Donald Hall offers a typical (male) critical response to *Tess of the d'Urbervilles*: 'Hardy was clearly in love with Tess, and he leaves his male readers in the same condition.'[4] Rosalind Miles' view of Hardy and women is typical of the second wave feminist criticism ('womanist' is a better term) which was pro-Hardy. For Miles, Hardy had an intuitive and exalted view of women:

> He had, surely, a deeply intuitive understanding of female nature… Hardy's guileless and ecstatic response to women in life irradiated his writing at every possible level… For Hardy really is a lover of women in the fullest physical sense. (1979, 25-26)

For some feminists, Hardy did not necessarily 'like' women, as (male) critics such as Irving Howe claimed (M. Childers, 1981).

A typical 'feminist' analysis of Thomas Hardy's work comes from Elaine Showalter. In "Towards a Feminist Poetics" (1979), Showalter offers a rather simplistic analysis of the wife-selling scene in *The Mayor of*

Casterbridge. She takes as her departure point one of the archetypal humanist studies of Hardy, Irving Howe's *Thomas Hardy* (1968).

> *What Howe, like other male critics of Hardy, conveniently overlooks about the novel is that Henchard sells not only his wife but his child, a child who can only be female. Patriarchal societies do not readily sell their sons, but their daughters are all for sale sooner or later.* (in M. Jacobus, 1979, 26f)

Showalter's analysis is in the same sort of vein as the feminism in Kate Millett's *Sexual Politics*. Millett's book deconstructed writers such as Henry Miller, Norman Mailer and D.H. Lawrence, exposing the sexist assumptions in their books. Millett's analysis, though, like much of Anglo-American feminism, is distinctly humanist, and modernist, assuming that whatever is in the text relates directly to the author, that whatever is in the text is there deliberately and consciously. This kind of Anglo-American feminism assumes that the text is transparent, so that if a text appears misogynist, then that writer is misogynist.

French feminism, cultural studies and postmodern feminism, however, does not regard the text as transparent, and departs dramatically from humanist criticism at many key points. Humanist feminism talks of Thomas Hardy, but postmodern or cultural theory feminism talks of 'Thomas Hardy', that is, a writer who is 'written' by the social, ideological, cultural, materialist and economic forces around 'him'. Feminism of the type of Millett, Showalter, Miles *et al* essentializes Hardy's female characters: this view of Rosalind Miles' is typical: '[f]or Hardy, femininity was a value, an essence, an eternal and inescapable fact' (1979, 43), which's patently untrue. Showalter's Anglo-American feminist analysis, then, is strong on simple assertions, but short on subtle, ironic, thoughtful insights. Showalter, for example, asserts:

> *Hardy's female characters in* The Mayor of Casterbridge, *as in his other novels, are somewhat idealised and melancholy projections of a repressed male self.* (ib., 26f)

Showalter assumes a direct line back from the character to the author. Roland Barthes has called for the 'death of the author', where the idea of the author who suffers for the book, who 'nourishes' the book, is discarded in favour of a notion of writing as a 'multi-dimensional space in which a variety of writings, none of them original, blend and clash' (R. Barthes, 1984, 144f). In cultural theory, 'writing' or 'literature' is multi-dimensional, with an infinity of possible readings. Linearity is discarded, and texts continually change. Nothing is fixed anymore, and meanings fluctuate.

You have to consider exactly what character is – a function of the text? What is the relation between character and text? A character is interpreted differently by everyone: how is a character constructed in the minds of different readers? What are the factors, 'inside' and 'outside' the text, that govern character?

Thomas Hardy's women are known and yet not known – by the reader (and, one suspects, by the narrator). Rather than getting to know the women in Hardy's novels, the reader gets to know Hardy's narrator (but not Hardy himself).[5] Female characters such as Tess, Eustacia, Sue and Bathsheba, seem to have a substantial and subtle subjectivity, but, as Judith Mitchell argues, their subjecthood is 'largely illusory' (ib., 179). Hardy's narrators offer detailed physical descriptions of the female characters, but leave out much of their thoughts. This is part of Hardy's narrational project, but it can also be seen as 'a glaring omission of female consciousness' (ib., 183). Hardy, via his narrators, gets up close and lovingly describes his heroines' physical features (most famously Tess's mouth), but his narrators are also oddly distanced from his characters. Consequently, Hardy's heroines remain mysterious, always partially unknowable by the reader.

There are moments, for example, when the reader would expect to find out what a female character is thinking: when Eustacia Vye is wandering the Heath just before her death, or Tess's feelings after she has killed Alec. Even in more mundane, less dramatic moments, such as when Marty puts down her billhook at the beginning of *The Woodlanders* and looks at her blistered hand, when the reader might expect to find out what she is thinking, the narrative moves into a more general voice.[6]

Patricia Stubbs pointed out that Thomas Hardy was ambivalent about his female characters, not always condemning the social pressures and psychological characteristics that contributed towards women's suffering (1979, 81f). Penny Boumelha reckoned that the radicalism of Hardy's depictions of women did not reside in their 'complexity' or 'realism' but 'in their resistance to a single and uniform ideological position' (1982, 7).

Hardy's novels were not always received favourably by women critics and readers. Hardy's own views, expressed outside of the novels, did not always square with those of feminists of the 1880s and 1890s. The ideological gap between Hardy and the women critics and feminists of the late 19th century is illustrated by Hardy's remark to Edmund Yates (in 1891): 'many of my novels have suffered so much from misrepresentation as being attacks on womankind' (*Collected Letters*, I, 250). Hardy hoped that works such as *Tess of the d'Urbervilles* would redress the balance.

In Thomas Hardy's fiction, as in so much of literature (certainly in the works of James Joyce, Norman Mailer, Henry Miller, D.H. Lawrence, Virginia Woolf, Gertrude Stein, Philip Roth, J.P. Donleavy) women and men are at odds with each other. The connection between men and women in fiction is always fraught with conflict. Luce Irigaray suggests a fundamental *difference* between the sexes: '[m]an and woman, woman and man are therefore always meeting as though for the first time since they cannot stand in for one another. I shall never take the place of a man, never will a man take mine.'[7] A politics of sexual union between men and women has still not been created, Irigaray suggests, because there is no continuity between the spiritual and material, the sacred and the sexual aspects of life.

> *A sexual or carnal ethics would demand that both angel and body be found together. This is a world that must be constructed or reconstructed. A genesis of love between the sexes has yet to come about, in either the smallest or largest sense, or in the most intimate or political guise.* (in ib., 127)

For Irigaray, as for Rainer Maria Rilke, the angel is the emblem or manifestation of a fluid openness, the angel is the one who opens up life, who circulates between God and humanity. One sees the 'angel' beginning to appear in *anima* or Sophia characters such as Sue Bridehead.

Lesbian, gay and queer cultural theory has continually addressed the problem of identity and gender. There are certain sexual and social 'positions' or 'categories' which are seen as 'outside' the (patriarchal) norms, which may have affinities with the female 'outsider' figures of Julia Kristeva and Luce Irigaray. The lesbian, for instance, is sometimes seen as an 'outsider', like the black woman, or the feminist. Gender and sexual identity categories are becoming increasingly blurred. For example, there are 'physical' lesbians, 'natural' lesbians, 'cultural' or 'social' lesbians, and 'male' lesbians (men who culturally position themselves as lesbians). There are men with vaginas and women with penises; there are queer butches and aggressive femmes, there are F2Ms and lesbians who love men, queer queens and drag kings, daddy boys and dyke mummies, transsexual Asians, butch bottoms, femme tops, women and lesbians who fuck men, women and lesbians who fuck *like* men, bull daggers, porno afro homos, lesbians who dress up as men impersonating women, lesbians who dress up as straight men in order to pick up gay men, butches who dress in fem clothing to feel like a gay man dressing as a woman, femmes butched-out in male drag and butches femmed-out in drag. Sexual/ social identities are continually being performed, blurred, re-defined, questioned. Terms such as 'straight' and 'gay', hetero and homo/ hommo, are no longer adequate for these multi-layered, postmodern sexual identities. As Judith Halberstamp puts it '[w]e are all transsexuals'.[8]

Some feminists regard sexuality as expressed through performances and gestures, rather than being some essence. Thus heterosexuality itself is not an unchanging 'institution', but may already be a 'constant parody of itself', as Judith Butler suggests (1990, 122). Heterosexuality, Butler reckons, is continually imitating itself, always miming its own performances in order to appear 'natural'. Further, if gender, sexuality and forms of sexuality such as heterosexuality are simulations and performances, the notion of a fixed, essentialist 'man' or 'woman' is no longer possible.[9] Catherine MacKinnon wrote: '[s]exuality is that social process which creates, organizes, expresses, and directs desire, creating

26

the social beings we know as women and men, as their relations create society.'[10] Adrienne Rich, in her influential essay "Compulsory heterosexuality and lesbian existence", says that heterosexuality is not 'preferred' or chosen, but has to be 'imposed, managed, organized, propagandized, and maintained by force'; for Rich, 'violent structures' are required by patriarchal society in order to 'enforce women's total emotional, erotic loyalty and subservience to men' (1980).

Thomas Hardy's female protagonists can be seen as characters struggling to attain coherent social and sexual identity, to become an independent body and soul, someone who can exist independently of a patriarchal culture. Critics have noted that figures such as Sue Bridehead are versions of the late Victorian 'New Woman'. Indeed, Sue proposes a number of feminist views, and *Jude the Obscure* is an early feminist work, in which relationships between the sexes and notions of gender are examined in the light of what Hardy might call 'progressive' philosophy. In *Jude the Obscure*, more than in any of his other works, Hardy grapples with the notion of an emergent 'New Woman', and a heartfelt proto-feminism.[11] At the same time, so-called 'New Woman' fiction was already going out of fashion when *Jude the Obscure* was published (1895); also, the 'New Woman' was not wholly feminist (P. Boumelha, 1982, 136-7).

One can see some of Hardy's other female protagonists as would-be feminists, as women struggling against patriarchy.[12] Each, in their own way, is trying to affirm her identity in the face of patriarchy. Tess, Marty, Eustacia, Elizabeth-Jane and Sue question, not always in obvious or outspoken ways, the rigours of patriarchy. Characters such as Tess, Eustacia, Sue and Elizabeth-Jane, in particular, are forms of 'woman' as 'outsider' figures who inhabit what feminists term 'the wild zone'. It's not perhaps surprising that Thomas Hardy should be so close to some aspects of contemporary feminism, in particular the notion of 'woman' as one of the marginalized, dispossessed people.

Feminists such as Elaine Showalter and Jeanne Roberts, taking their cue from Edwin Ardener,[13] propose that there is a female 'wild zone', as there is a male 'wild zone'. We know about men's version of wild zone eroticism, it's the place of 'glorious phallic monosexuality', in Hélène

27

Cixous' words.[14] The female 'wild zone' is beyond patriarchal space, beyond patriarchal representations.[15] Julia Kristeva and Luce Irigaray, among other French feminists, have spoken of something in 'women' or the 'feminine' that is 'unrepresentable', beyond art, beyond male culture. In *About Chinese Women*, Kristeva writes of the woman as a witch, someone outside of patriarchal discourse, or at least, thrown to the edge, the border between the known zone and the wild zone:

> *...woman is a specialist in the unconscious, a witch, a bacchanalian, taking her* jouissance *in an anti-Apollonian, Dionysian orgy. A* jouissance *which breaks the symbolic chain, the taboo, the mastery. A* marginal discourse, *with regard to the science, religion and philosophy of the* polis *(witch, child, underdeveloped, not even a poet, at best his accomplice). (The Kristeva Reader, 154)*

Tess Durbeyfield is called a 'witch' by Alec, but the meaning here is witch = whore (the 'Witch of Babylon'). Eustacia Vye is not only likened to a witch, she is physically attacked by Susan Nonsuch, who pierces her in church with a needle, echoing the 'pricking' of witches in mediæval times. Sherry Ortner writes that 'woman is being identified with – or, if you will, seems to be a symbol of – something that every culture devalues'.[16] Ann Rosalind Jones describes Julia Kristeva's notion of the 'outsider' culture of women, of women as 'witches':

> *Women, for Kristeva... speak and write as "hysterics," as outsiders to male-dominated discourse, for two reasons: the predominance in them of drives related to anality and childbirth, and their marginal position vis-à-vis masculine culture. Their semiotic style is likely to involve repetitive, spasmodic separations from the dominating discourse, which, more often, they are forced to imitate.[17]*

Julia Kristeva's writings may be the most coherent and incisive account of the psycho-cultural 'wild zone'. Victor Burgin, describing Kristeva's philosophy, says that she positions

> *the woman in society... in the patriarchal, as perpetually at the boundary, the borderline, the edge, the 'outer limit' – the place where order shades into chaos, light into darkness. The peripheral and ambivalent position*

allocated to woman, says Kristeva, had led to that familiar division of the field of representation in which women are viewed as either saintly or demonic – according to whether they are seen as bringing the darkness in, or as keeping it out.[18]

Saintly woman (the Virgin Mary is a typical example) keeps the amazing energy of the female wild zone out of men's lives; the demonic woman (Mary Magdalene, the *femme fatale*, vampire, 'devil woman') is the one who brings the wildness with her. Patriarchy of course prefers bland, mute, passive door-stops in women, people who will stop the darkness from coming in, who will sit there and say nothing and get on with society's housework. For Julia Kristeva, Christianity offers a limited number of ways in which women can participate in the 'symbolic Christian order': for the woman who is not a virgin or a nun (like Hardy's heroines), who is sexual, has orgasms and gives birth

her only means of gaining access to the symbolic paternal order is by engaging in an endless struggle between the orgasmic maternal body and the symbolic prohibition – a struggle that will take the form of guilt and mortification, and culminates in masochistic jouissance. *For a woman who has not easily repressed her relationship with her mother, participation in the symbolic paternal order as Christianity defines it can only be maso-chistic.* (1986, 147)

This applies to Thomas Hardy's characters such as Sue Bridehead and Tess. Two of the classic ways in which women have been allowed to participate in Christianity is the *'ecstatic* and the *melancholy'* (ib.).

André Breton said that 'existence is elsewhere'. French feminists say that 'woman' is elsewhere. 'She is indefinitely other in herself,' writes Luce Irigaray, maintaining that women

are already elsewhere than in the discursive machinery where you claim to take them by surprise. They have turned back within themselves, which does not mean the same thing as 'within yourself'. They do not experience the same interiority that you do and which perhaps you mistakenly presume they share.'[19]

Here, perhaps, in the female 'wild zone', some of the wildness and strangeness and ecstasy of 'female' eroticism may be experienced and depicted. Luce Irigaray also spoke in spatial terms of idealist feminism (it's all about labia for Irigaray):

> We need both space and time. And perhaps we are living in an age when time must re-deploy space. Could this be the dawning of a new world? Immanence and transcendence are being recast, notably by that threshold which has never been examined in itself: the female sex. It is a threshold unto mucosity. Beyond the classic opposites of love and hate, liquid and ice lies this perpetually half-open threshold, consisting of lips that are strangers to dichotomy. Pressed against one another, but without any possibility of suture, at least of a real kind, they do not absorb the world either into themselves or through themselves, provided they are not abused or reduced to a mere consummating or consuming structure. Instead their shape welcomes without assimilating or reducing or devouring. A sort of door unto voluptuousness, then? Not that, either: their useful function is to designate a place: the very place of uses, at least on a habitual plane. Strictly speaking, they serve neither conception nor jouissance. Is this, then, the mystery of female identity, of its self-contemplation, of that strange word of silence; both the threshold and reception of exchange, the sealed-up secret of wisdom, belief and faith in every truth?[20]

For some feminists, Luce Irigaray's morphology of female creativity is empowering, 'a challenge to the traditional construction of feminine morphology where the bodies of women are seen as receptacles for masculine completeness.'[21] Other feminists see the emphasis on just one form of female sexuality as a distinctly reductive and inauthentic kind of feminism:

> If we define female subjectivity through universal biological/ libidinal givens [writes Ann Rosalind Jones], what happens to the project of changing the world in feminist directions? Further, is women's sexuality so monolithic that shared, typical femininity does justice to it? What about variations in class, in race, and in culture among women? about changes over time in one woman's sexuality? (with men, with women, by herself?) How can one libidinal voice – or the two vulval lips so startlingly presented by Irigaray – speak for all women? (1986, 369)

Many feminists suggest that women's eroticism cannot be represented, much as women themselves cannot be represented. Julia Kristeva writes:

'[i]n "woman" I see something that cannot be represented, something that is not said, something above and beyond nomenclatures and ideologies.'[22] Other feminists echo this idea, that women cannot be fully represented in the traditional media of patriarchy. As Hélène Cixous writes:

It is at the level of sexual pleasure in my opinion that the difference makes itself most clearly apparent in as far as woman's libidinal economy is neither identifiable by a man nor referable to the masculine economy.[23]

The unrepresentable in art and pornography, according to some feminists, is women's eroticism, their *jouissance*, that 'explosive, blossoming, sane and inexhaustible *jouissance* of the woman', as Julia Kristeva describes it.[24]

What one gets in most Western art, from Greek and Roman sculpture through the glories of the Renaissance to the latest pornography are male representations of female eroticism. Feminists say that there are no real depictions of female *jouissance* in art or literature. 'In my opinion,' writes Marguerite Duras, 'women have never expressed themselves.'[25] What she means, perhaps, is that women have expressed themselves thus far in terms and means defined by men. There is no 'feminine' or 'women's' writing, according to some feminists. Hélène Cixous reckons she's found only three 'inscriptions of femininity' this century: Sidonie-Gabrielle Colette, Marguerite Duras and Jean Genet.[26]

The point is *not* to consider bodies as essential or absolute, for 'no "body" is unmediated'.[27] In *écriture féminine* the body is a major source of creative energy, so that 'to write from the body is to recreate the world' (A. Jones, 1986, 366). Real sex, the French feminists argue, has not yet been represented. Women haven't done it because they work within the same patriarchal structures, codes and constraints as men. Men, generally, haven't got a hope of depicting authentic 'female' eroticism, although the authors of millions of pornographic products would claim they know everything about 'female' eroticism. On the other hand, in the mechanisms of cultural/ postmodern theory, anyone, male or female, should be able to create a truly 'feminine' text. It shouldn't matter who the author is. If the French feminists are right, then nearly all of the art produced anywhere is orientated to the male and the masculine, even when it is created by women. Many women artists would dispute this. The notion of an 'authentic' 'women's'/ 'feminine' art continues to be hotly debated.

According to the French feminists, 'women's' or 'feminine' or 'female' art is created in the gaps and silences of a text, but not in the intentional space of the artwork. Mary Jacobus explains:

> The French insistence on écriture féminine – on woman as a writing-effect instead of an origin – asserts not the sexuality of the text but the textuality of sex. Gender difference, produced, not innate, becomes a matter of the structuring of a genderless libido in and through patriarchal discourse. Language itself would at once repress multiplicity and heterogeneity – true difference – by the tyranny of hierarchical oppositions (man/woman) and simultaneously work to overthrow that tyranny by interrogating the limits of meaning. The 'feminine', in this scheme, is to be located in the gaps, the absences, the unsayable or unrepresentable of discourse and representation.[28]

Some feminist critics, such as Gayatri Chakravorty Spivak and Emma Pérez, believe that 'representation cannot take place without essentialism'.[29] For some feminists, philosophies based on the body are problematic, because to look for some essential nature of 'woman', some essence based in biology is dubious.[30] Indeed, Toril Moi writes that 'to define 'woman' is necessarily to essentialize her.'[31] What is 'woman', anyway? A 'writing-effect', for the feminist Alice Jardine, an element in culture or a text. It's important, as Monique Wittig notes, to make a distinction between the various interpretations 'woman' and 'women':

> Our first task... is thoroughly to dissociate "woman" (the class within which we fight) and "woman," the myth. For "woman" does not exist for us; it is only an imaginary formation, while "women" is the duct of a social relationship.[32]

Sue Bridehead and Jude's non-marital state disrupts the conventional notions of sexual relationships in late 19th century society. There are even more disruptive erotic relationships possible, though, such as homosexuality and lesbiansim. Even more potentially 'subversive', as far as heteropatriarchy is concerned, are lesbian motherhood, or sexual representations between crossdressing, transvestite or transsexual partners.

There is no erotic relationship in Thomas Hardy's fiction that approaches such unorthodoxy or fucking with gender, and there's only one representation that's seen as 'lesbian' by Hardy critics (Miss Aldclyffe and Cytherea Graye in *Desperate Remedies*). Describing Miss Aldclyffe's reaction to Cytherea helping her undress, a (male) Hardy critic says that Miss Aldclyffe's rigid body and firmly closed mouth 'is how a forty-six-year-old sexually excited woman in such a situation would behave' (M. Seymour-Smith, 1995, 129). What a ridiculous pronouncement.

There are other relationships between women which Thomas Hardy critics, if coaxed, might admit have some lesbian elements: Grace and Felice lost in the woods and clinging to each other, their dialogue becoming more and more intimate; and Tess and the 'sisterhood' at Talbothays and Marlott. Gay male eroticism can be discerned in many of the friendships in Hardy's fiction. This often occurs when lovers of the same woman meet and commune in the 'trade' of women between men that Luce Irigaray identified (Wildeve and Venn; Oak and Boldwood). In Hardy's fiction, only mild forms of 'gender-play', 'gender bending', 'gender-fucking' or 'fucking with gender' occur.[33]

The sexual relations in Thomas Hardy's fiction overwhelmingly conform to the heteropatriarchal model. Anything non-monogamous or adulterous is viewed with horror by some parts of the Wessex community. What is surprising, perhaps, is the number of feminists in the early 21st century who also believed in (heterosexual) monogamy as the goal. Even for some radical feminists, lovers still have to be wholly committed to monogamy.[34] Men must not be interested in other women. They are not even allowed to look at pictures of naked women – this is seen as tantamount to adultery. 'I should be everything for him', the devoted wife complains when she finds pornography in her husband's cupboard. But, Christobel Mackenzie asks, '[w]hat can this possibly have to do with the real relationships people have?'[35] That is, looking at pornography is one thing, but does it mean a total breakdown in the relationship? Or looking at other people, perhaps with desire? Hardy's fiction explores this heterosexism, which states that heterosexual couplism must be the norm, with the total devotion of each partner to the other. One is not allowed to glance at anyone else, or speak about them. Having no relationship is no good either: the individual is soon hounded by society to conform and marry. Thus, Bathsheba, when Troy's buggered off, has Boldwood on one side waiting patiently but tremulously for her signal to agree to wed him after six years, and Oak on the other side, waiting even more patiently, and threatening to leave for California. In *Desperate Remedies* the narrator's bitter comment applies to many of the later Hardy heroines (Grace with Fitzpiers, Tess with Alec, Bathsheba with Troy):

> *Of all the ingenious and cruel satires that from the beginning till now have been stuck like knives into womankind, surely there is not one so lacerating to them, and to us who love them, as the trite old fact, that the most wretched of men can, in the twinkling of an eye, find a wife ready to be more wretched still for the sake of his company.* (16. 4)

As one critic notes, while for Thomas Hardy's men the crisis may be intellectual or ethical, for Hardy's women it 'is always sexual in nature'.[36]

THOMAS HARDY AND WOMEN'S ART

Creating (a) 'feminist æsthetics' means writing / rewriting language, art, culture, notions of knowledge and ontology, of identity and politics, all manner of things. For Julia Kristeva, there is no 'other place' in language, for, as Ludwig Wittgenstein said, the world people live in is a world circumscribed by language. In effect, language 'writes' the world: to go beyond it is the quest for the 'wild zone', the utterly Other Place. For Kristeva, revolution must occur *within* symbolic (that is, patriarchal) language.[37] Women's writing or art becomes a literature of absence, of negative capability, revealing by what it does not reveal, forever outside yet also inside patriarchal discourse. As the Marxist-Feminist Literature Collective write:

Women, who are speaking subjects but partially excluded from culture, find modes of expression which the hegemonic discourse cannot integrate. Whereas the eruptive word cannot make the culturally inaccessible accessible, it can surely speak its absence. Kristeva has classified these modes of existence as 'semiotic' as opposed to 'symbolic'.[38]

'When women use *je* as the subject of a sentence, this woman *je* most often addresses a man and not another woman or women. It does not relate to itself either' writes Luce Irigaray (1994, 46).

Julia Kristeva asks questions which are central to feminist æsthetics and 'women's' art. Will there be a visionary feminism which takes women's art (French feminists use the term 'writing' to cover cultural/ creative activities) into a new era?

Or is it, on the contrary and as avant-garde feminists hope, that having started with the idea of difference, feminism will be able to break free of its belief in woman, her power, her writing, so as to channel this demand for difference into each and every element of the female whole, and, finally, to bring out the singularity of each woman, and beyond this, her multiplicities, her plural languages, beyond the horizon, beyond sight, beyond faith itself?[39]

Kristeva is very positive, though, despite her insistence on absence. She is uncompromising; in "Freud and Love" she says she believes in the 'notion of emptiness, which is at the heart of the human psyche'.[40] Yet she is optimistic, too. Her philosophy is founded on absence, yet she often writes of the possibility that a 'wild zone' or otherness has been neglected, that there maybe a nighttime space, of the unconscious, of magic or otherness. In Thomas Hardy's fiction night scenes are prominent, times and spaces where the unusual, the marginal and the magical can be manifested. Many of the key moments in the erotic lives of Hardy's characters occur at night, when objectivity and rationality is blurred by ambiguity and desperation. In *Women's Time* she asks more questions:

Is it because, faced with social norms, literature reveals a certain knowledge and sometimes the truth itself about an otherwise repressed nocturnal, secret and unconscious universe? Because it thus redoubles the social contract by exposing the unsaid, the uncanny? (The Kristeva Reader, 207)

And, again from *Women's Time*, Kristeva argues for aspects of female subjectivity that could exist outside of patriarchy:

> *As for time, female subjectivity would seem to provide a specific measure that essentially retains* repetition *and* eternity *from among the multiple modalities of time known through the history of civilizations. On the one hand, there are cycles, gestation, the eternal recurrence of a biological rhythm which conforms to that of nature and imposes a temporality whose stereotypes shock, but whose regularity and unison with what is experienced as extra-subjective time, cosmic time, occasion vertiginous visions and unnameable* jouissance. *On the other hand, and perhaps as a consequence, there is the massive presence of a monumental temporality, without cleavage or escape, which has so little to do with linear time (which passes) that the very word 'temporality' hardly fits: all-encompassing and infinite like imaginary space, this temporality reminds one of Kronos in Hesiod's mythology, the incestuous son whose massive presence covered all of Gaea in order to separate her from Ouranos, the father.* (ib., 191)

Language is central to the creation of a 'feminist æsthetics'. Women are denied the place to really *speak*, as many feminists note. Luce Irigaray remarked:

> *When a girl begins to talk, she is already unable to speak off/to herself. Being exiled in man's speech, she is already unable to auto-affect. Man's language separates her from her mother and from other women, and she speaks it without speaking in it.*[41]

In *The Woodlanders*, Grace Melbury, like many other Thomas Hardy heroines, does not have men's deftness with language. The narrator says that '[s]he could not explain the subtleties of her feelings as clearly as he [her father] could state his opinion' (XXII). Firm masculine opinion or fact is set against feminine subtlety which verges on the inarticulate. The poet, in a sense, writes inside the mother, or from the mother, or from the maternal realm. 'The poet's *jouissance* that causes him to emerge from schizophrenic decorporealization is the *jouissance* of the mother' writes Kristeva (1986, 192). But why, Kristeva asks, 'is the speaking subject incapable of uttering the mother within her very self? Why is it that the "mother herself" does not exist?' And why, Kristeva adds, is the mother only phallic? (*Desire in Language*, 194).

Biographers and critics of Mr Hardy have long remarked upon his witnessing of two hangings. The first one occurred on August 9, 1856, when the 16 year-old Hardy saw Martha Brown hanged. The sight apparently deeply impressed Hardy. The erotic component, related in the *Life* – seeing her 'tight black silk gown' accentuating her figure – was also evident, according to Hardy's biographer. 'No boy of sixteen could have escaped being affected by the ghastly juxtaposition of sex and death' (commented Martin Seymour-Smith, 33). It wasn't just sex and death that were combined, it was sex, death and *looking*. In the *Life* Hardy feels guilty for witnessing the hanging.

The intense scopophilic element was also in evidence in the other execution Hardy witnessed. While living at Bockhampton, he heard about the hanging taking place in Dorchester at eight in the morning. He went onto the heath with a brass telescope to see it. Just as he put the 'scope to his eye he saw the white figure falling.

> *The whole thing had been so sudden* [he writes in the *Life*], *that the glass nearly fell from Hardy's hands. He seemed alone on the heath with the hanged man, and crept home wishing he had not been so curious.*

It is the last sentence that speaks of the intensity of the experience – he felt alone on the heath with the hanged man, there was a sense of total identification with the victim, with the drama of the execution. After the intensity, comes the guilt at having witnessed the event; Hardy reacts like people who gleefully watch horror films then wish afterwards that they hadn't: the images of violence often persist. Somehow, Hardy realizes, by deliberately going out onto the hill to see the execution, he was implicated in it. The sight of it connects him to the victim, the gallows, the executioner, the officials and the crowd watching. Young Tom Hardy becomes a Peeping Tom. The intensity of this event is emphasized by Hardy's visual description of it: the sun behind him shining on the white gaol, with the 'murderer in white fustian' and the officials in dark clothes. The next step biographers and critics usually make is to connect these experiences of execution to Tess's, which's witnessed from a distance. Feminist critics have noted, though, that what is specifically *not seen* is Tess's hanging, her body in its final grotesque act. Instead, the flag indicates her death. What is significant about Hardy and the executions he witnessed were that he *saw* them, and was guiltily fascinated with them. The ideology of the Lacanian gaze is very much at work in these memories related in the *Life*. One sees them not only in Tess's death, but in most of Hardy's work. As Luce Irigaray says, women remind men of their own body, mortality and nature. Susan Griffin wrote 'a woman's body, by inspiring desire in a man, must recall him to his own body'. This is the age-old linking of women with sex and death.

In the œdipal complex, when the father enters the mother-child dyad, a series of displacements occur and the mother becomes the perpetually lost object (J. Kristeva, 1982, 62f). 'Distance from the 'origin' (the maternal)' writes Mary Ann Doane, 'is the prerequisite to desire; and insofar as desire is defined as the excess of demand over a need aligned with the maternal figure, the woman is left behind' (1987, 173). In her essay on Hardy's early novels, Judith Wittenberg speaks of the 'voyeuristic moment' in Hardy's fiction, when the 'seeing subject and the seen object intersect in a diegetic node that both explicitly and implicitly suggests the way in which the world is constituted in and through the scopic drive' (1983, 151).

One can see how important looking or voyeurism is in Thomas Hardy's fiction, for voyeurism is founded on keeping a spatial distance between subject and object, as Christian Metz noted.[42] Distancing encourages eroticism, because the system of representation – an image of a woman standing in for the real woman – makes the reality less threatening. And, importantly, representations of the erotic object (women) are easier to manipulate to suit one's own ends than 'real' women, as Hardy's male characters know well.[43] Hardy's lovers love from a distance, but when they behold the beloved up close, their desire withers. When the Hardy lover finally unites with the beloved, the former dissatisfaction returns. 'With contact loves dies' (J. Miller, 1970, 176).

For French feminists such as Hélène Cixous, the philosophy of the Lacanian 'lack' is ridiculous. As she writes in "The Laugh of the Medusa": '[w]hat's a desire originating from a lack? A pretty meagre

38

desire' (E. Marks, 262). And Luce Irigaray and other feminists (Koman, Grosz, Montrelay, Doane) have criticized the Freudian-Lacanian emphasis on the phallus as the 'transcendental signifier', as the measure of authentic sexual pleasure.[44] What woman lacks is lack itself, says M. Montrelay, an inability to create distance and representation (Tess is denied this).

From Plato to Freud and Lacan the desire/ lack has been central to Western sexual metaphysics: in this negative model, one is doomed to a desire for more and more consumption, which leads to dissatisfaction. The 'lack' or emptiness at the heart of Hardy's lovers can only momentarily be filled. Erotic plenitude never lasts (J. Miller, 1970, 184). Freudian-Lacanian desire can never be satisfied: dissatisfaction is built-in. Desire is never annihilated: for Georg Wilhelm Hegel, only another desire can satisfy desire and also perpetuate it. Desire thus desires more desire (this has a vivid expression in late capitalist consumerism, where it is always the *next* commodity that will truly satisfy and stop the hunger for more objects. But it never happens).

Another way of looking at desire is not to see it as the (unattainable) search for satisfaction stemming from a lack (Jacques Lacan), nor as related to denial and prohibition (Sigmund Freud), but rather as a positive force of fullness and production, that creates interactions, that makes connections between things. Instead of internalization and obliteration (Hegel), desire may join and make things (Friedrich Nietzsche and Benedict Spinoza). For Gilles Deleuze and Félix Guattari (*pace* Spinoza and Nietzsche), desire is a positive force, 'inherently full. Instead of a yearning, desire is seen as an actualization, a series of practices, action, production' (Elizabeth Grosz).[46] As Hélène Cixous says: 'my desires have invented new desires' (E. Marks, 246).

The poetic moment, for Julia Kristeva, is founded on desire: desire is what keeps the system together:

The other that will guide you and itself through this dissolution is a rhythm, music, and within language, a text. But what is the connection that holds you both together? Counter-desire, the negative of desire, inside-out desire, capable of questioning (or provoking) its own infinite quest. Romantic, filial, adolescent, exclusive, blind and Oedipal: it is all that, but

39

for others. It returns to where you are, both of you, disappointed, irritated, ambitious, in love with history, critical, on the edge and even in the midst of its own identity crisis. (Desire in Language, 165)

In "Psychoanalysis and the Polis", Kristeva's comments on desire chime with the course of desire delineated in Thomas Hardy's fiction:

Desire, the discourse of desire, moves towards its object through a connection, by displacement and deformation. The discourse of desire becomes a discourse of delirium when it forecloses its object, which is always already marked by that 'minus factor' mentioned earlier, and when it establishes itself as the complete locus of jouissance (full and without exteriority). In other words, no other exists, no object survives in its irreducible alterity. (1986, 308)

The Lacanian Look emphasizes eroticism. Seeing is erotic, the eye becomes a kind of phallus, caressing the obscure object of desire, which it can never 'possess'. As the poet Rainer Maria Rilke wrote '[g]azing is a wonderful thing.'[47] The act of looking eroticizes the object. The Look is an assertion of male power and sexuality. 'Male desire is presented as a response to female beauty' states Andrea Dworkin (*Intercourse*, 114). This is how Alec d'Urberville responds to Tess when he first meets her: it is her beauty, he thinks, that inflames him, and he can do nothing about abating his desire. Margaret Whitford glosses Luce Irigaray's work thus:

Western systems of representation privilege seeing: what can be seen (presence) is privileged over what cannot be seen (absence) and guarantees Being, hence the privilege of the penis which is elevated to the status of the Phallus. (30)

Lacanian psychoanalysis is a hell of misrepresentations and mis-readings, mirrors and imaginary spaces. The subject in the Lacanian system is constantly trying to make good mistakes made in its early psychosexual growth. In the dreaded mirror phase, the image becomes a mirage, and a distance is set up between the image and the body, an absence which Lacan termed the *objet a*. In the confusions of the three realms, the symbolic, real and imaginary, the subject cannot realize what it most wants to realize. The objects of desire remain forever elusive (like

Angel Clare longing for Tess, and vice versa).

There is something inexplicably depressing about Lacan's version of psychosexual events. Lovers, in the Lacanian system, desire what they cannot have. The problem of the lack, the *objet a* and *la chose*, can never be resolved. Lacanian philosophy posits, among other things (here we go): an eternal search for what can never be found.[48] The Freudian-Lacanian system demands a continuous series of substitutions for the objects to fill the primordial lack. It is a system of replacing an imaginary and immobile plenitude that will always fail. The primal realm remains always lost or forbidden. The Paradise of early childhood recedes ever further into the distance of the past.

In the Jungian system, Beatrice, Laura, Cleopatra, Isolde, Eurydice, Ariadne and all those women of myth, poetry and legend, are incarnations of the *anima*, which is, as Carl Jung explains, something all males possess: '[e]very man carries with him the eternal image of woman, not the image of this or that particular woman, but a definitive feminine image.'[49] The *anima* is 'a personification of the unconscious in a man, which appears as a woman or a goddess in dreams, visions and creative fantasies', write Emma Jung and Marie-Louise von Franz.[50] Male writers throughout history have depicted their version of the *anima*, it seems. Each (male) writer has a version of the 'inner feminine figure' as Jung calls her (1967, 210-1). For artists, this idealized *anima* figure seems to be another manifestation of that obscure object of desire, the eroticized woman, a mirror for male lust. The equation is: the more sublime and voluptuous the woman is depicted, the more sublime and voluptuous is the artist's desire.

In Thomas Hardy's fiction, characters such as Sue, Tess and Eustacia Vye have a powerful *anima* component for their male suitors. Bridehead is clearly an *anima* figure for Fawley: his first sight of her is an *anima* vision, framed by the trappings of Christianity and the glow of stained glass. Jude's vision of Sue recalls Dante Alighieri seeing Beatrice Portinari in the little church in Florence, recounted in the *Vita Nuova*.

Further: in Lacanian psychology, desire, which is the foundation of the system, is enmeshed with speaking, with creativity and art. The œdipal crisis and the repression of the desire for the mother occurs with the entry into the Symbolic Order, and the entry into language. As Toril Moi

41

crystallizes Lacan's thought so concisely: '[t]o speak as a subject is therefore the same as to represent the existence of repressed desire' (1988, 99-100). Men gaze at women and manipulate them into erotic poses (Jude with Sue, Alec and Angel with Tess, Wildeve and Clym with Eustacia, Henchard, problematically, with Elizabeth-Jane). Larysa Mykyta writes:

> The sexual triumph of the male passes through the eye, through the contemplation of the woman. Seeing the women ensures the satisfaction of wanting to be seen, of having one's desire recognized, and thus comes back to the original aim of the scopic drive. Woman is repressed as subject and desired as object in order to efface the gaze of the Other, the gaze that would destroy the illusion of reciprocity and oneness that the process of seeing usually supports. The female object does not look, does not have its own point of view; rather it is erected as an image of the phallus sustaining male desire.[51]

The same social and ideological forces that operate in Thomas Hardy's novels are at large in the contemporary Western world. A Lady Jayne fashions advert in a mid-1990s 'woman's magazine', for example, shows a woman and a man about to kiss, in colour and close-up, over two pages. The copy to this heterosexual, romantic (and ethnically white) ad echoes the Lacanian pleasure of looking in Hardy's fiction:

> One look, THE look, and you know you're in for an enchanted evening. It starts with beautiful hair, irresistibly dressed with fashion accessories by Lady Jayne. It ends with a kiss... Or perhaps rather more?[52]

The 'rather more' here means romance, a relationshiop, and fucking, of course. In other words, with the help of Lady Jayne hair fashions one might end up fucking someone at the end of the evening. A night which begins with 'beautiful hair' might end with 'rather more', i.e., 'heterosexual intercourse'. Throughout women's magazines (all magazines, all media), one sees these bourgeois romantic scenarios at work, where, at the end of the evening, tupping is the apotheosis, the 'happy ever after' ending of fairy tales, the delicious icing on the cake, the ultimate way of 'rounding off' a night out. It's a yawn, but Cinderella myths sell products.

The most intense sequence of erotic looking in Thomas Hardy's fiction occurs in the opening of *Far From the Madding Crowd*. Here is the classic Lacanian scenario of a man looking at a woman without her knowing. The Lacanian/ filmic undercurrent is exaggerated when Bathseba Everdene takes out a mirror and looks at herself, smiling. The language depicts erotic pleasure – Bathsheba has her eyes half-closed, parts her lips and smiles, and blushes profusely. The narrator even reminds the reader of the novelty of the event taking place outdoors, instead of in a bedroom (chapter I). When Oak confronts Bathsheba, returning her hat, Hardy's narrator makes the power of phallic voyeurism explicit:

> *Rays of male vision seem to have a tickling effect upon virgin faces in rural districts; she brushed hers with her hand as if Gabriel had been irritating its pink surface by actual touch...* (III)

The intensity of Lacanian desire and Freudian projection is underlined at the end of chapter II when Gabriel Oak is described as having a lack or void inside him:

> *Having for some time known the want of a satisfactory form to fill an increasing void within him, his position moreover affording the widest scope for his fancy, he painted her a beauty.* (II)

Jude has the same lack inside him after seeing Arabella for the first time: before meeting her, he didn't know it was there. Similarly, before Gabriel meet Bathsheba, he is reasonably content. Her arrival makes him realize his life is not complete without a woman.

43

The pleasure of the text, whether the text is a painting, film, magazine, photograph, piece of theatre, and so on, comes, according to Roland Barthes, when the Look of the spectator is aligned with that of the author.[53] Judith Wittenberg speaks of Thomas Hardy's 'spectatorial narrator' (1983, 152). What feminist criticism has done is to question the masculine 'pleasure of the text', arguing for a feminist reading of the traditional masculine or patriarchal view of texts. This debate has been central to feminism's approach to Hardy's fiction – the problem of the gender of the narrator and spectator. 'Hardy's narrators persist in constructing and interpreting female characters according to standard notions about woman's weakness, inconstancy, and tendency to hysteria' commented Kristin Brady.[54]

For some feminists, there can be no true 'feminist gaze', because the Look is always masculine, ultimately. If the spectator is a 'gendered object', suggests Annette Kuhn, then 'masculine subjectivity [is] the only subjectivity available' (A. Kuhn, 1982, 63). The politics of representation, which are central to the consumption of culture and art, are weighted firmly in favour of men and patriarchy. As John Berger writes: 'men act and women appear'. Catherine King notes: 'most images in masculine visual ideology are created to empower men as spectators – that is, to see themselves as endlessly important with things laid out for their desire'.[55]

Post-Lacanian feminists such as Luce Irigaray argue that subjectivity can only be attributed to women with difficulty. Irigaray claims that 'any theory of the subject has always been appropriated by the 'masculine'' (*Speculum*, 133). 'Woman' is tied to a 'non-subjective subjectum' (ib., 265). Irigaray stresses the sexed being, the sexualized subject and speaking position. No form of knowledge or philosophy can be authentic or 'universal' if it ignores the 'female' position.

Irigaray concentrates on the act of enunciation, the act of producing discourse. Irigaray stresses the interiority of the speaking subject, the traces of subjectivity found in acts of communication. The continual denial of a sexualized discourse threatens the possibility of an emergent non-patriarchal society. Irigaray has investigated the use by men and women of everyday language, concluding that men and women privilege different patterns of speech, with men encouraging their 'self-affection', or relations to/ with the self and the self projecting in others, while women use language to make connections and relationships with both sexes. Irigaray's deconstruction of the languages of science, philosophy and politics has demonstrated the repression of the feminine – Dale Spender and other feminists have come to similar conclusions. For Irigaray, this repression is not in-built into language, but reflects the (patriarchal) social order. In order to change one the other must also be changed.

Luce Irigaray's argument fits in exactly to a feminist reading of Thomas Hardy's fiction, in particular of *Tess of the d'Urbervilles* as a study of the relations between speaking, language, sexuality, identity, power and patriarchy. Irigaray says that if the vagina is regarded as a 'hole', it is a 'negative' space that cannot be represented in the dominant discourse. Thus to have a vagina is to be deprived of a voice, to be decentred or culturally subordinated, and so Irigaray replaces Lacan's mirror with a vaginal speculum.[56]

One feminist critic of *Tess of the d'Urbervilles* puns Tess's 'wholeness' with her 'holeness', that is, Tess as sexual lack or vagina waiting to be filled by the male characters and the reader gendered as male by the narration.[57] The phallic privileging of the masculine 'I' (penis, phallus, power, identity, soul – Alec and Angel) means that female sexuality is rendered 'invisible', just as the vagina is a negative space or void (Tess). The phallus is the divine, beloved mirror, emblem of masculine narcissism ('"You are Eve, and I am the old Other One"' mocks Alec in chapter 50). But the vagina, being a 'black hole', can reflect back nothing. There is no self there. Male speculations and narcissistic gazes create a male subject: the mistakes arise when this male subject is equated with the whole world. This occurs in the perception of Alec and Angel, who cannot comprehend realms of sexuality and ideology outside of the phallocentric, patriarchal norms. The universality of philosophy and psychoanalysis thus becomes founded on a one-sided (male) view of the world (the narrator in Hardy's novels also ambiguously embodies this view). Male sexuality and narcissism mistakenly becomes the basis for the universal model of sexuality of psychoanalysis. Female sexuality becomes the negative image of male sexuality, if female subjectivity is considered at all (Sue Bridehead and Tess Durbeyfield continually deny their own sexual desires). Women are supposed to have 'penis envy', a hankering for the transcendent signifier which will enable them to attain a positive, creative identity. Freudian 'penis envy' has been rejected by most feminists.

One can see how Luce Irigaray would have upset Jacques Lacan, who founded his theory of sexuality, like Sigmund Freud, on the primary of the phallus. In the Freudian-Lacanian phallic system, all is unity, identity, singularity (going all the way back through history to that initial 'singularity', the Big Bang). Ambiguity, multiplicity and excess are excluded from this view: Luce Irigaray's project of rewriting Freud and Lacan disrupts the isomorphic unity and replaces it with a series of dense, poetic, parodic discourses, in which female repression is unleashed and the female unconscious is allowed to explode into academic patriarchy. Irigaray's specular project disrupts the insistence in phallic, patriarchal sexuality on one organ (penis), one orgasm or pleasure (male), one identity (male), one model of representation (masculine). Irigaray's notion of 'feminine writing' disrupts the unitary dimensions of the phallocratic system ('there would be no longer be either subject or object' Irigaray wrote of the new 'female syntax' in *This Sex Which Is Not One*, and 'oneness' would no longer be privileged' [134]).

For some feminists, Luce Irigaray's rewriting of Lacan is still as essentialist as Lacan's phallic discourse; for others, Irigaray's specular discourse is not essentialist, for 'Irigaray is nobody's fool, [and] not Lacan's'.[58] Some critics who are more sympathetic to Irigaray's thought (M. Whitford, N. Schor, J. Gallop, E. Grosz, J. Féral, C. Burke, D. Fuss) offer a more sophisticated reading than those feminist critics (T. Moi, M. Plaza, J. Sayers, A. Jones) who see nothing but essentialism in Irigaray's philosophy (C. Weedon, 1987, 63; D. Stanton, 1986, 160; M. Plaza, 1978; J. Sayers, 1986, 42; B. Brown, 1979, 38). Irigaray, though, emphasizes not so much biological as morphological feminist strategies: her emphasis is very much on forms of representation of the body, and how these modes of representation relate to society and social ethics. It is the social inscription of corporeality, not the anatomical body in itself, that is important.

Luce Irigaray writes that '[m]en always go further, exploit further, seize

46

more, without really knowing where they are going' (*Thinking*, 5). This is certainly seen in the behaviour of self-confident, socially able men in Hardy's fiction, such as Edred Fitzpiers, Alec d'Urberville and Captain Troy: they embody the colonizing, territorial, phallic tendency Irigaray describes. It can't be simply a case of 'blaming' men for everything, as Simone de Beauvoir said – blame men, yes, but also blame 'the system' (society). Luce Irigaray thinks that the abstraction 'equality' can only mean *at best* the equality of salaries, so that women will be paid the same as men; nothing else, Irigaray says, can be 'equal'; instead, there must eternal *difference*, in gender, from the sexual to the cultural. Irigaray says that difference must be emphasized, but her theory of difference is based, like the metaphysics of Andrea Dworkin, on sexuality. Sexuality lies at the heart of the feminist discourse of feminists such as Dworkin, Irigaray, Hélène Cixous, Kate Millet, Susan Griffin and Shere Hite; they emphasize sexuality more than other factors, and this is a problem, this reduction, ultimately, to sexual matters. Donna C. Stanton has criticized Cixous' theories, seeing in them a return to the metaphysics of presence and identity, in which the technique of poetic metaphor suggests an economy of similitude, instead of one of difference (D. Stanton, 1986).

Luce Irigaray's views on 'gender equality' revolve around notions of women's sexual difference:

The demand to be equal presupposes a point of comparison. To whom or to what do women want to be equalized? To men? To a salary? To a public office? To what standard? Why not to themselves? (1993, 12)

For Irigaray, the exploitation of women derives from sexual difference, so the solution, she says, 'will only come through sexual difference' (1993, 12). Women's oppression and exploitation, says Irigaray, is incredible, bearing in mind where men come from.

We still live in a framework of familio-religious relations in which the woman is the body to the man's head. It's quite astonishing that men, whom in their cradle were totally dependent upon women and who owe their existence to this dependence, should then take the liberty of turning things around: men exist thanks to women's intelligence, but apparently women aren't capable of governing society or even of being full citizens... In an incredibly distrustful manœuvre, it's suspected that they would no longer want to protect life the moment they themselves have a right to it. Women are often nothing more than hostages of the reproduction of the species. (1993, 78)

The trouble is that all Thomas Hardy's characters are 'victims', 'victims' of the eternal urge towards marriage which society/ culture breeds in people. But as nearly all feminists say, marriage is a step in the wrong direction. As Simone de Beauvoir says:

Then refuse marriage if possible… When you are married, people see you as married, and you begin to see yourselves as married. This is quite different from the relationship you have with society when you are not married. Marriage is dangerous for a woman.[9]

Marriage takes away from women their economic power, their sexual power, their power to work, their identity, so many things. Don't get married! Many feminists say it. And Thomas Hardy does too, but his viewpoint is that marriage ruins love, whereas the feminists state that marriage ruins a lot more than love. It ruins money, economy, labour, sexuality, identity and politics.

For Simone de Beauvoir, feminism must be an economic revolution which destroys the injustices of the class system. So her recipe for success is economic independence:

To be really independent, what counts is to have a profession, to work. It means that when you are married, if you wish to divorce, you can leave; you can support your child; you can make a life for yourself. But work is not the solution for everything. It has both liberating and dehumanizing aspects. (in ib., 147)

Thomas Hardy shows how difficult it is for women to have economic independence. With the character of Tess, he explores a woman on her own, a woman cast off by men and patriarchy, yet, ultimately, remaining dependent on men and patriarchy. Tess works – she really works, hard – but still she cannot be successful. *Tess of the d'Urbervilles* is a rigorous materialist analysis of the economic situation of women in the late 19th century. *Tess of the d'Urbervilles* bears up well to an in-depth feminist and

Marxist/ materialist analysis, for, like *Madame Bovary*, it exposes many of the hypocrisies of patriarchal culture. The problem is that women are seen by men as possessions, things to 'have', to 'take' ('have' and 'take' are typical terms for sex – indeed, Hardy plays upon the horror of possession in *The Woodlanders* when Grace Melbury finds out Mrs. Charmond has slept with Fitzpiers, and she cries '"You've had him!"').

Wildeve desires Eustacia Vye again when he finds out that another man wishes 'to possess her' (III. vi). Luce Irigaray says women are seen by men as merchandise: '[w]omen, signs, goods, currency, all pass from one man to another'.[59] And this is exactly what happens in Hardy's novels, in most novels: the women are 'traded' by the men, and the mark of possession, of 'buying' a woman, is to fuck her. Sex stamps 'possession' on the woman, as Andrea Dworkin points out:

> *Male sexual power is the substance of culture. It resonates everywhere. The celebration of rape in story, song, and science is the paradigmatic articulation of male sexual power as a cultural absolute. The conquering of the woman acted out in fucking, her possession, her use as a thing, is the scenario endlessly repeated, with or without direct reference to fucking, throughout the culture. (Pornography, 23)*

This happens in Thomas Hardy's fiction: Tess Durbeyfield is 'traded' between Angel and Alec, and is 'possessed' by both. Alec 'possesses' Tess physically, sexually, and Angel 'possesses' her sexually too, though by not sleeping with her. His possession works by a negation of eroticism, which, in the Christian way, still upholds the sexual status quo of patriarchal power-gaming. Angel emphasizes her virginity, which reinforces the sexual status quo, which men dictate, and Alec emphasizes her eroticism, which also reinforces the status quo. Tess is seen as both virgin and whore by her 'men', much as the Goddess Aphrodite was both whore and virgin, and in Christianity there is the double aspect of the Mother of God: the virginal Mary and the prostitute Mary Magdalene. In other words, Alec screws Tess and possesses her, Angel doesn't screw Tess but still possesses her.

Grace Melbury, Bathsheba, Susan Henchard – these women are defined by their men. Only a few women in Thomas Hardy's fiction have their own identities, largely free from men's definitions (though defined by patriarchy in general): Eustacia, Sue Bridehead, Tess, Elizabeth-Jane. There are many more men with independence, of course.

Marion Wynne-Davies, discussing Elizabethan England, writes:

Woman as a physical entity to be possessed and controlled with sexual, familial and political discourses, as well as in the metaphoric figures of city, state, empire and the earth itself, is seen to be consumed by the patriarchal ideologies of late sixteenth century England.[60]

In Hardy's fictive world, women are always operating within and being defined by patriarchy. And if women move outside of patriarchy, as Tess and Sue try to do, they get punished. Jean E. Howard defines ideology as 'the obviousness of culture. What goes without saying, what is lived as true',[12] and one can see in Hardy's narratives the obviousness of the male-slanted, men-orientated society, the patriarchal rules of the game.

The sexual, economic, political, cultural and ideological status quo is upheld, reinforced and dictated by the men and women in Thomas Hardy's fictions. When people question this establishment, they are derided, outcast, punished. The system is that women stay at home and look after the house and the family and the children, and the men do the work outside, make the external decisions, and so on. Men in Hardy's world, and men in general, want women to stay in their place. D.H. Lawrence was scared of 'cocksure women', of domineering women. Many writers have been frightened of powerful women. Hardy likes them, but shows how difficult a time they have of it.

There is something in women that men cannot control, and men hate this. There is something wild, perhaps, or 'other', or different, which men cannot grasp or contain. And men absolutely loathe not being in control. As Julia Kristeva, says:

In "woman" I see something that cannot be represented, something that is not said, something above and beyond nomenclatures and ideologies.[62]

In Tom Hardy's fiction, as in most fiction, men are active, women are passive, men act, and women are acted upon. When this duality is abolished, when women try to usurp this status quo, they are punished, and the duality, the two-tier hierarchical system, with men always on top, is reasserted even more forcefully.

'Men desire women because their gender role positions them as active; women desire men because their own 'lack' must be filled,' writes Valerie Traub in "Desire and the Difference It Makes".[63] In Hardy's narrative world, both men and women desire marriage and love because they feel an intense lack. Without love they are lonely, or, worse, nobody. Love gives them an identity, and a purpose in life. So they desire love out of desperation, because without love they are not whole. They are not truly themselves, they lack an identity. For Eustacia Vye, marriage seems to be a way out, a gaining of identity and fulfilment. But of course, marriage is not these things. It is another form of prison, and Hardy demonstrates this in all his fictions. Identity and social standing are gained in marriage. This is rubbish, of course, but is still so much the view today. In desiring marriage, the protagonist is merely exchanging one form of prison for another.

III

Love, Sex and Marriage
in Thomas Hardy's Fiction

Though fervent was our vow,
Though ruddily ran our pleasure,
Bliss has fulfilled its measure,
And sees its sentence now.

Ache deep, but make no moans:
Smile out; but stilly suffer:
The paths of love are rougher
Than thoroughfares of stones.

Thomas Hardy, 'The End of the Episode' (CP, 227)

Early on in his writing career, at the time of *The Poor Man and the Lady,*
Thomas Hardy recognized the importance of erotic desire in fiction: 'as a
rule no fiction will considerably interest readers rich or poor unless the
passion of love forms a prominent feature in the thread of the story'.[1]
Hardy's characters yearn so painfully – Eustacia Vye cries out for a great
love to help her escape. 'To be loved to madness – such was her great
desire' (121). Love – the great yearning – proves to be her downfall. She
dies for love, like Cathy Earnshaw in *Wuthering Heights.* Hardy's women

yearn, but rarely do they get an earthlover like Heathcliff. Intense love means intense death. Love now but die later – this is the Romantic credo. The love between Clym Yeobright and his mother is equally intense, and destructive. It reaches a profundity of painfulness (VI. i). Tess lives, for a season, in 'spiritual altitudes' which are ecstatic (XXXI). Her tragedy is also Eustacia Vye's and Marty South's – her yearning for love is not reciprocated. Love is not returned, passion burns itself away and is thrust out from the soul into the darkness of the universe. The self is ultimately alone – the modernist post-Romantic stance.

The narrator of *Jude the Obscure* (and also Phillotson) sees Sue and Jude as two halves of one whole – a Gnostic love-union of selves (*Jude*, IV. iv), which is called the *syzygy* in Gnosticism. In fact, their togetherness is very shaky. The dialectic of their love is continually shifting – from desire to disgust, and all the shades in between. There is no easy, simple dualism of reciprocation for Hardy. Sue and Jude drift apart and come back together in waves. They fuse then fragment, like particles in some sub-atomic experiment. It is a bout of Empodeclean Love and Strife for them, a state of Heraclitean flux, a Hegelian neurotic tension, with the world-weary detachment of Arthur Schopenhauer added.

In Sue and Jude the big themes – the pagan and the Christian, the traditional and the modern, the spiritual and the sexual – are at war. Thomas Hardy depicts love-in-flux, always being modulated, changed, destroyed, rebuilt, transfigured. Sue and Jude fly together involuntarily – such as in their kiss on the silent road, when they 'kissed close and long' (IV. iii). But soon they fall apart again. The pattern was laid down long ago in figures of myth such as Isis and Osiris, Ishtar and Tammuz, Anna and Baal, and in the later figures such as Anthony and Cleopatra, Héloïse and Abélard, and Petrarch and Laura. Hardy's narrators are heretical about love. They do not believe in marriage. Their ideas on love have much in common with the mediæval cults and heresies: of courtly love, the Cathars, Templars, Sufism, Albigensian heresy, alchemy and the cults of the Grail and the Black Virgin. Though it is not as strident as in some writers, there is in Hardy's fiction the urge towards spiritual sublimation, the transcendence of the flesh and the mysticization of the erotic.

Love in Mr Hardy's world is about two people trying to 'follow their bliss' (Joseph Campbell's term). In Hardy's novels the urge of the lovers is to escape, to find, like Sue and Jude, Angel and Tess, their own niche in the world, away from other, interferring people. Hardy put it utterly plainly and so passionately in his poem 'The Recalcitrants':

> *Let us off and search, and find a place,*
> *Where yours and mine can be natural lives,*
> *Where no one comes, who dissects and dives*
> *And proclaims that ours is a curious case,*
> *Which its touch of romance can scarcely grace.*
> (*Complete Poems*, 389)

This is the great dream of lovers – to re-create the world and to find a place in which to really live and breathe. The problem is that society and all kinds of other factors subvert this lust for loneliness. 'Love is the burning-point of life' says Joseph Campbell (*Power*, 205) and the tragedy of Hardy's novels, as D.H. Lawrence notes in *Study of Thomas Hardy*, is that the pioneers in love die in the wilderness (21).

Escape, but die. Remain, and live. The Kierkegaardian risk-taking is everything. Without risk there is no life. Life is lived on the edge. This risk-taking for the glory of love is the main theme in Hardy's fiction. The way he deals with it makes him 'great' – as with Fyodor Dostoievsky or William Shakespeare or Sappho. 'His feeling, his instinct, his sensuous understanding is, however, apart from his metaphysic, very great and deep, deeper than that perhaps of any other English novelist' remarked Lawrence (*Study of Thomas Hardy*, 93).

Thomas Hardy's fiction is full of supernatural sensibilities. He conversed many times with his dead wife, Emma: '[w]ould that I lay there | And she were housed here! | Or better, together | Were folded away there | Exposed to one weather | We both...' ('Rain on a Grave', CP, 441). The Hardy-poet yearns to be united with his decayed lovers, in the Emily Brontëan manner: '[t]he eternal tie which binds us twain in one | No eye will see | Stretching across the miles that sever you from me' (CP, 421). The romantic idea of lovers meeting over distances, or at night, in dreams, or after death, extends the Western notion of the soul to its logical extreme. One aim of the writer is to make writing like love – to write and love, to make the act of writing love itself, to make desire concrete in art, the two fusing, love and art, into one life. The aim is to fuse life and love and art. As Hardy wrote in his poetry: '[l]ove lures life on' ('Lines', in CP, 458).

One of Sappho's short lyrics on love reads:

It brings us pain
and weaves myths.[2]

This describes concisely the dominant discourse of love in Hardy's (and most) fiction: the Nietzschean/ Christian emphasis on suffering, and the subsequent myth-making. (Sappho is quoted in *Jude the Obscure*, though with a different meaning – referring to Sue Bridehead in the epigram to 'Part Third, 'At Melchester').

Love in Thomas Hardy's work is Keatsian and Shelleyan. Hardy's work is fleshly, sensuous but also doomed. His love-affairs take much of their flavour from poems such as John Keats' 'La Belle Dame Sans Merci'. Elfride, in her vanity, asks Stephen from her pony in *A Pair of Blue Eyes*: '"Do I seem like La belle dame sans merci?"' (57). The reference probably suggested itself to Hardy as he constructed this scene. The fairy queen/ knightly lover motifs feature also in the romances of Bathsheba and Oak, Sue and Jude, Eustacia and Clym. The dark sensualism of Keats is well suited to Hardy's work. Hardy is a slave to love, as a poet, as he is a slave to women, to Woman, like poets such as Dante Alighieri, Francesco Petrarch, John Donne, Robert Herrick and Robert Graves. Hardy's women are Muses who throw down enchantments over the initiate's soul and senses. Hardy's beloveds are the Symbolist and Decadent Fatal Women, the pale wraiths eulogized by poets such as Charles Baudelaire, A.C. Swinburne and Samuel Taylor Coleridge, and by Franz von Stuck. Gustave Moreau and Félicien Rops in painting. Robert Graves had his Laura Riding, as Hardy had his Emma Gifford. The poetry records a haunting of the poet-alone by the Elf-Queen. The antecedents of this scenario are many – the classic one in English literature being of course Shakespeare and his formidable Dark Lady, she '[w]ho art as black as hell, as dark as night' (last line of sonnet no. 147).

Another ancestor is Merlin's enthrallment at the hands of Ninue. In the poesie of John Keats and Percy Bysshe Shelley and the Elizabethan poets we find the powerful spirit of Arthuriana, embodied in figures such as the Lady of Shalott or Morgan Le Fey, before they became trivialized in late Victorian poetry and Pre-Raphaelitism. These romantic ideas surged throughout Europe in the late 12th century and afterwards with the troubadours. But England was late in incorporating Arthurian legend. The new concepts and *mœurs* of love and individualism took hold in the Elizabethans. In Thomas Campion's exaltation of the 'fairy queen Prosperina' for instance. Nothing new about these sorcerous Madonnas, however. Giraut de Borneil, Arnaut Daniel, Bernard de Ventadour and the other troubadours, *jongleurs* and minstrels had all done it before, and so well, too. William Shakespeare is the apotheosis in English literature of this kind of love-poetry. Romanticism is the end of it all – though a wild, chaotic and intense kind of death.

Thomas Hardy arrives at the very tail-end of this extended demise. What is raised up in his love-poetry is the authenticity of his experience and poetic voice. Hardy is not as violent, nor as high-flown, as the Elizabethans. Nicholas Breton wrote in *The Passionate Shepherd*: 'to kill love's maladies, | Meet her with your melodies' (in G. Hiller, 244). This is the answer – when stabbed to death by love, re-birth yourself in art, in love-poetry. Or as Keats would have it:

> ...*if thy mistress some rich anger shows*
> *Emprison her soft hand, and let her rave,*
> *And feed deep, deep upon her peerless eyes*[3]

Thomas Hardy's poetic persona is not as assertive as Keats or Shakespeare, though there is still the same masochistic misogyny in some of his poetry. The Hardy lover though, like Shakespeare, wants to be slain by his beloved. 'Kill me outright with looks', implores the Shakespearean poet, while Jude, at the terrible climax of his romance with Sue, also implores his black Mistress:

> *"Don't go – don't go!... This is my last time! I... shall never come again.*

Don't then be unmerciful, Sue, Sue! we are acting by the letter, and the letter killeth!" (Jude the Obscure, VI. viii)

The letter, the vicious law of a dying religion, Christianity, certainly does kill. So the poet begs for *merci*, that key blessing in Renaissance and chivalric love-poetry. But the poet knows it is useless – it is all over, just as Tess cries, but hopelessly '"Have Mercy!"' (XXXV) The romances of Jude-Sue have a Shelleyan subtext to them. They are built upon an ætherealizing orientation of spirit-over-sex. Shelley's poem 'When Passion's Trance is Overpast' forms the philosophical basis of Hardy's romances:

If it were enough to feel, to see
Thy soft eyes gazing tenderly,
And dream the rest – and burn and be
The secret food of fires unseen,
Could thou but be what thou hast been.[3]

Love without touching, sex through spirituality, a deeply sensuous love-act transcending skin and ordinary sense – this is a common ambition in Hardyan Wessexuality. Think of all those poems of Hardy's, in which the poet meets some beloved by night, but they do not touch or kiss, just talk. Hardy aims to spiritualize love, but in a heterodox, not doctrinal, manner. *Jude the Obscure* records the failure of this sacralization of love, its near-impossible fusion with everyday domestic and economic life. Hardy's holy love, like Shelley's, needs a sacred, secret place away from other people, in which to flourish. But there's none left. So one has to create one's own – and how difficult that is. Hardy's lovers aim to do this: '[l]et us off and search, and find a place' Hardy wrote in 'The Recalcitrants'. But they fail. Robert Herrick wrote the same pæan: '[c]ome, let us go while we are in our prime' (in 'Corrinna's Going-a-Maying'). It is an anti-social ambition, an escapism in love almost wholly unrealizable.

Thomas Hardy is very bitter about this secular failure to recapture an earlier hermetic love-time. In his poem 'She to Him I' he wrote: '[t]hat Sportsman Time but rears his brood to kill' (CP, 15). This is the bleak view of Tess, who wishes she'd never been born into this cynical game of the gods. Hardy tries to look honestly and clearly at life – to go after the 'offensive truth' (Per, 26). His pessimism is really 'evolutionary meliorism' (ib, 52). As he says in the poem 'In Tenebris': 'if a Better way there be, it exacts a full look at the Worst' (CP, 168). Hardy depicts people full of 'fret and fever' (Per, 42), the idea is 'given the man and woman, how to find a basis for their sexual relation' (ib, 19). Hardy quotes his beloved Shakespeare in support of his claims: 'life [is] time's fool' (Per, 47, quoting *King Henry* iv i, V, iv, 81). The flipside is '[l]ove's not Time's fool' (sonnet no. 116).

The work of Shakespeare and Hardy is the result of the attempt to fuse these two viewpoints – the hopeless and the idealistic. Love's not time's fool, but life is – how typically of two realist and often determinist artists to be so ambivalent. They know love and life and art and time and death cannot be simply reconciled. In both Hardy and Shakespeare Time marches on, unstoppable, even though, sometimes, it 'must have a stop'. No. It eats everything away, demolishing all as it sweeps by. Wes-sex-mania ends up as a drowned body in a heathland river (*The Return of the Native*), or a hanged woman in Winchester goal (*Tess of the d'Urbervilles*), or a derelict dying in Oxford (*Jude the Obscure*), or a corpse in a Dorset wood (*The Woodlanders*).

How desolate Thomas Hardy's view of the outcome of love seems to be. He is an optimist blasted by life's shocks into bitter realism. His works record satires of circumstance, life's little ironies and time's laughingstocks, those human shows with their few moments of vision, offensive truths hidden amongst post-pastoral Wessex tales.

How forlorn Thomas Hardy actually is can be adjudged from the endings to his tragic novels, and throughout his poetry. Tragedies must end in death, it seems (but how awful and ludicrous is Viviette's collapse at the end of *Two on a Tower*). There is much doom and gloom in the poetry. It is there in the early poems – in 'Neutral Tones', for example. Hardy's imagery in this short lyric is bleak, while the poem's sparseness looks forward to Samuel Beckett: the white sun, dead pond, barren earth (these are stage-settings for *Waiting For Godot* or *Happy Days*). Hardy rages here, too, though in a quiet way – the poet learns that 'love deceives' and thus the sun, the innocent, utterly non-human sun, becomes 'God-curst' (CP, 12). This is typical of the love-poem in the West: the jilted lover must have the outside world reflect his/ her desolation.

The futile scene in 'Neutral Tones' is picked up in Hardy's last novel – it forms the opening of *Jude the Obscure*. Jude, the 'natural boy', works in the 'wide and lonely depression of the empty field' (I. iii). The depth of Hardy's rage is clear from the way he develops this scene – Jude soon gets beaten up by Farmer Troughton, and whirled around like a toy. The target of Hardy's anger is made explicit – it is not God, nor the birds nor nature, but the human world in which Jude lives (I. iii).

Thomas Hardy is bitterly ironic in his use of Percy Shelley as one of the major discourses in *Jude the Obscure*. Hardy counters his grim realism with a Shelleyan aching for sweetness and release. It is this quivering yearning that powers Eustacia Vye, Tess Durbeyfield, Sue Bridehead and Jude Fawley, and also Pierston in *The Well-Beloved* in his Platonic search for a Shelleyan 'Beloved'. Eustacia, Tess and Sue are Shelleyan heroines, yearning for a delicacy of touch and spirit that the workaday world simply cannot provide. The gulfs between the two form the tension at the heart of the Hardy novel (*Life*, 272). These conflicts force the Hardyan anti-hero to cry, with Shelley: 'O World, o Life, o Time'.

Thomas Hardy can be seen as ultimately an optimist. He does weave in an escape-clause at the end of his novels, most prophetically (and ambiguously) in the figures of Angel and Tess's sister, as a New Adam and Eve. And in 'The Darkling Thrush', with its heartfelt synthesis of the poetry of Keats, Shelley and Wordsworth, Hardy rejoices that out of the waste land a bird can still sing, and that 'there trembled through/ His happy good-night air/ Some blessed Hope' (CP, 150).

The Promethean rebellion in Thomas Hardy's fiction occurs in sexual politics and erotic desire. For Hardy's disaffected, dispossessed, depressed and often displaced characters, the way out is through/ by / in/ with love. In Hardy's fictive world, religion no longer offers moments of ecstasy and union, but love, the 'profane' experience, still does. What Jude Fawley does is what all Hardy's lovers do: he creates a religion of love around Sue, what Stendhal called the 'crystallization of love'.[4] The problems arise because there is a gulf between the individual's wishes and what society demands of the individual. What Jude does is to build up a cult or religious aura around Sue, and the more it's built up, the greater his fall will be. Aunt Druisilla recognizes the danger of such erotic objectification and warns Jude against it. Jude has to realize, and it's painful, that Sue will not conform to his psychic projection of her as a virginal essence. In the Godless world of Hardy's lovers, the beloved has to stand in for divinity, much as the lady of courtly love poetry was a divinity akin to the Virgin Mary. However, no individual can replace God or divinity, and the result is always disillusion for Hardy's lovers.

American Jungian Joseph Campbell wrote of marriage:

> *There are two stages* [of marriage]. *First is what I call the biological stage which has to do with producing and raising children, and the other is what I would the alchemical marriage – realizing the spiritual identity that the two are somehow one person. It is the image of the androgyne, the male/female being. That is the image of what is being realized through a marriage. In that mythological reference the two are one. (This business,* 22)

Thomas Hardy's couples rarely even get to the physical/ sexual/ parental stage, let alone the spiritual/ alchemical stage. Often they are in a rush to be spiritually fused, and ignore everything else. They trip up. The sexual/ domestic level is so problematic that the spiritual/ emotional side has no hope of working out successfully. In Thomas Hardy's world of love, the two-in-oneness is continually scuppered by the demands of sexuality, materialism, economics, politics and society. In Hardy's fiction, 'weddings be funerals', as Widow Edlin put it in *Jude the Obscure*. Marriage is called wed*lock*: Arabella brandishes the 'padlock' of wedlock (her wedding ring) to her neighbours in her second marriage with Jude. It's usual for tragedies to end with death, while romances, fairy tales and comedies climax with marriage. In Hardy's fiction, tragedies often begin with marriage, while the 'pastoral' or 'romance' novels always contain marriage. Interestingly, Hardy described Tess's condition in the latter part of the narrative as being a living death: for Hardy, Tess is a 'mere corpse drifting with a current to her end' (E. Blunden, 1942). A curious way to regard one's favourite heroine, but typically Hardyan.

The alchemical 'two-in-oneness' is most powerfully evoked in *Jude the Obscure*, but it occurs throughout his work, as throughout Western culture.

There is always the hope that, somewhere, somehow, at some time, a sexual love can be united with a spiritual love. It is this desire for a unity of sex and spirit as well as two lovers, that lies behind *Romeo and Juliet*, Dante's *Vita Nuova*, Petrarch's *Canzoniere*, John Donne's *Songs and Sonnets* and Emily Brontë's *Wuthering Heights*. Hardy's lovers believe, against all the odds, in the spiritualization of love. They know the sexualization of love, this is what provides the stories with much of their dramatic tension. Love exists in a nostalgic past or in a never-to-be-attained future. 'The *meeting*, then, mixing pleasure and promise or hopes, remains in a sort of future perfect' writes Julia Kristeva.[5]

The relation between love and language for Kristeva pivots around primary narcissism:

> ...*when one transposes into language the idealization on the edge of primal repression that amatory experience amounts to, this assumes that scription and writer invest in language in the first place precisely because it is a favourite object – a place for excess and absurdity, ecstasy and death. Putting love into words... necessarily summons up not the narcissistic parry but what appears to me as narcissistic economy.* (*Tales of Love*, 267-8)

Writing of love perpetuates the 'narcissistic economy'.[6] To explore her psychoanalytic theory of love, Kristeva often employs the tactic of setting things against each other, of opposites. Thus, she explores the realm of the obverse of love – hate. This is another reason, perhaps, why Hardy turned from novels to poetry, because poetry may be closer to his idea of turning writing into love. Making writing *of* the (love) experience the experience itself. This idea has a correspondence with the French feminists, with Hélène Cixous and Luce Irigaray, who speak of the *jouissance* of writing, of the sexuality of the text. Hélène Cixous speaks of literary texts which deal with 'libidinal education'. Cixous' description of these works corresponds to Hardy's *Tess of the d'Urbervilles, Jude the Obscure, The Return of the Native, The Mayor of Casterbridge* and many others:

> *We have worked on a group of texts which belong to what can be called the literature of apprenticeship, the* Bildungsroman, *and all of the texts – and there are a lot of them because literature is after all their domain – which*

relate the development of an individual, their story, the story of their soul, the story of their discovery of the world, of its joys and its prohibitions, its joys and its laws, always on the trail of the first story of all human stories, the story of Eve and the Apple. *World literature abounds in texts of libidinal education, because every writer, every artist, is brought at one moment or another to work on the genesis of his/ her own artistic being. It is the supreme text, the one written through a turning back to the place where one plays to win or lose life.*[7]

On one level, artistic creation counters Lacanian lack and Kristevan absence: the act of writing staves off emptiness and loneliness by filling up the psychic space. As Julia Kristeva wrote in *Freud and Love: Treatment and Its Discontents*:

If narcissism is a defence against the emptiness of separation, then the whole contrivance of imagery, representations, identifications and project-ions that accompany it on the way towards strengthening the Ego and the Subject is a means of exorcising that emptiness. (1987, 42)

At the same time, the author's characters can provide much amusement, even a kind of spiritual solace.

Thomas Hardy's novels are explorations of love and its relation to identity, self, soul, politics, class, gender, and so on. Hardy's characters try to discover the inside of the people they love. But the beloved other always remains a mystery. The mystery, however, does not prevent the intense yearning. Mystery only aggravates desire.

The mystery is that I do not understand the beings that I love the most [writes Hélène Cixous], *and that even so that does not prevent me from either loving them or understanding them: what I do not understand is their own mystery, which not even they themselves reach. But I know their incomprehensibility well.*[8]

The trouble is, in getting close to another person, all manner of social and psychological problems arise. Or as Hélène Cixous puts it: '[t]here is an apple, and straight away there is the law' (1994, 133). With the apple comes the law: Eve (women) is punished, Cixous says, because she has access to the inside, to pleasure, to touching. Eve

is punished since she has access to pleasure, of course a positive relation-
ship to the inside is something which threatens society and which must be
controlled. That is where the series of "you-shall-not-enter" begins. (1994,
134).

In *Jude the Obscure* it is 'woman's nature' which 'breaks' up Sue and the
Sue-Jude relationship – Jude is not ruined by 'man's nature' because
'man's nature' is 'a term and concept that had no currency in the
nineteenth century.'[9]

Hardy's novels so graphically explore the desire and the prohibition,
the lust for life and the laws that come down like walls of steel around the
soul.[10] One sees this agony of desire and fear so clearly in books such as
Jude the Obscure and *The Mayor of Casterbridge*, where the apple of
temptation is dangled before the protagonists, then the problems begin. At
the end of *Two on a Tower* the apple of life is brutally torn away from
Swithin's grasp as Viviette dies in his arms. So close, yet so far away: so
much presence, and yet the agony of absence. Hélène Cixous writes:

It is the struggle between presence and absence, between an undesirable,
unverifiable, indecisive absence, and a presence, a presence which is not
only a presence: the apple is visible and it can be held up to the mouth, it is
full, it has an inside. (ib., 133)

Tess Durbeyfield is of course the character most obviously likened to
Eve. And Tess finds out that the punishment is brutal for those who eat the
apple. As soon as the apple appears, the prohibitions appear, the long list
of 'thou shalt nots', as Sue Bridehead bitterly knows. Pleasure, in Hardy's
world, as in the Christian West, is punished.

"Domestic laws should be made according to temperaments, which should
be classified. If people are at all peculiar in character they have to suffer
from the very rules that produce comfort in others!"' (233)

Part of the problem in Hardy's fictive world of desire is that only one
particular person will do. In *Sebastian*, Lawrence Durrell writes:

Every girl's a one-man girl, and every man too. Hence the trouble, for just
anybody won't do – it's gotta be the him and the her of the fairy tale.[11]

Hardy's lovers won't have anybody else except The One in their sights. All their desire is aimed at one person, and an alternative person won't do. For Jude it must be Sue, for Tess it must be Angel, for Marty it must be Giles, and so on. As American filmmaker Bette Gordon observed, '[u]sually the object of your obsession is less important than the fact of being obsessed.' It's the obsession that counts.[12]

If there were a magic formula or potion to make someone love you, the Hardyan lover would do anything to buy it. In fact, Vibert the quack doctor in *Jude* does sell a love potion, but it is not of course the Grail. Hardy's lovers live on the edge. They are artists of desperation. Desire in Hardy's fiction creates dishonesty: the greater the desire, the more willing the protagonist is to achieve their desire. As John Kucich puts it, 'dishonesty is simply one of the desperate remedies of desire'.[13] The deeper the desire, the greater the risks, and potential rewards. Characters in love become increasingly desperate. Desire entraps the protagonist (often they don't recognize their entrapment), and also produces a desire to entrap other people, especially other lovers.

In *The Woodlanders* Fitzpiers tells Giles, concerning Grace Melbury, that he is in love with '"something in my own head, and no thing-in-itself outside it at all"' (XVI). In Jungian terms, Thomas Hardy's male characters have to learn how to integrate the 'feminine' side of themselves, how to discern between the *anima* and the projection of their desires and needs onto other people. Hardy's male protagonists have to assimilate the feminine, a process which is problematical and painful. Henchard, Angel, Jude and Giles find it a real struggle to identify with and assimilate the feminine.

Joseph Campbell writes:

The problem of therapy is to bring the "head" into harmony with the energies that are informing the body, so the transcendent energies can come though. Only when this occurs are you transparent to transcendence. This implies yielding yourself to nature; putting yourself in accord with nature and, I would say, that is the main aim of most of the mythologies of the world. (This business, 25)

This is another way of putting the basic problem in Thomas Hardy's novels, which D.H. Lawrence called the problem of 'coming into being'. Hardy's people are not 'transparent to transcendence', rather, they are earthbound, and continually concentrate on a symbol instead of seeing through it. They are supremely literal. Like children, they have to have results *now*, and physically in front of them. Think of Grace and Giles, or Sue and Jude, or Tess and Angel, how childish they are, how they cling onto a literal interpretation of events. Joseph Campbell writes of the *Bible*, which forms such a large part of the literary-cultural background of Hardy's fiction:

> ...*the Bible is a compendium of all the mistakes that have ever been made in the translation of symbolic forms into historical forms.* (ib., 44)

What Campbell means is that people mistake the 'mask' of God for God himself. They think the *Bible* is 'literal', that the miracles really happened. They miss the metaphoric nature of religion. Thomas Hardy's lovers are the same: they mistake the symbol for the thing itself. Desperate, Hardy's lovers grasp at any sign and analyze it, turning it into something much more than it is. Eustacia, stuck on Edgon Heath, grasps at anything that might enable her to escape. Hardy's lovers do not recognize the metaphoric aspect of spiritual love. For them, love must have a physical, literal, conscious manifestation. Critics do the same: they read Hardy's fiction literally, seeing in his novels a series of literal events.

The problem of being transparent or opaque to transcendence is at its most acute in *Jude the Obscure*, where the lovers fight to have their kind of supra-sexual, proto-spiritual love accepted by society. They fail, partly because society (in this case the neighbours in Oxford/ Christminster) cannot see that love between a man and woman who appear to be married does not have to be sexual. It is the very appearance of a non-sexual bond, one that, further, has not been sanctified by society and law and the church, that incenses Sue and Jude's neighbours. William Greenslade suggests that Sue and Jude could refute biological determinism and 'make their own sexuality the medium of self-definition: the text might then utter what it suppresses but continually intimates' (181).

Sue and Jude try to explore an area where heterosexuality, let alone sexuality, is not 'compulsory'. As feminists have noted, not only is heterosexuality socially and ideologically 'compulsory', in Adrienne Rich's phrase, but sexuality is compulsory: everyone is expected to be sexual, to be sexually active.[14] 'Women are expected to be in, or to want to be in, a sexual relationship'.[15] You see this so clearly with Tess Durbeyfield: Tess's mother is but the first of many people who expects Tess to desire a sexual relationship. Witness Alec's astonishment when she rejects him: *what?* he implies, *you don't desire me?* But not just women: everyone is expected to be sexual.

In the radical feminist terminology of Andrea Dworkin, Susan Griffin, Kate Millett and others, being 'sexual' is equated with being fucked. In the patriarchal system, in the view of some feminists, women cannot win: they are condemned if they don't want or have sex, but women who express their sexuality are regarded with suspicion. As adolescents, what is seen as 'natural' for boys to express, sexually, is criminal for girls. Women who admit to liking sex are 'somehow seen as 'dirty' or 'bad'; this happens to Hardy's female characters: '[w]e are so afraid to be seen as 'whores' that we accept the idea of ourselves as 'victims' if we have sex. All this does for women is make being a victim seem natural' remarked Becky Rosa.[16] Alec calls Tess a whore in order to justify his seduction of her. Being seen as a 'victim' limits women, and may render them 'inert by self-pity'.[17] Being a prostitute may be the only way in which women are allowed to express themselves sexually in a fiercely patriarchal society. Thus, Alec calls Tess a whore to align himself with patriarchal culture. Christianity divides women into two basic sexual types: the Virgin Mary, the saintly, worshipped Mother, or Mary Magdalene, the whore. Tess may be seen as a latter-day form of the ancient 'holy whore', the sacred prostitutes who served Goddesses such as Cybele and Isis. What's clear is that Tess is not allowed to be both, mother and sexually active woman.

No one, in life or art, it seems, can escape from being defined by their sexual identity and activity. Thus, everyone is branded socially by what they do sexually: so, old people are defined by their sexual *in*activity and jokes are made about the non-performance of their genitals. In the media, in magazines and TV programmes, in films and radio shows, people are depicted either in or not in a sexual relationship, and the sexual relationship takes precedence over all others, over friendship, over being a child or a parent, over business and social relationships. Everyone is expected to be in, or to want to be in, a sexual relationship, and when someone isn't interested, the media hounds them, by making fun of them, by lampooning the individual's non-sexual status. One sees this so clearly in Thomas Hardy's fiction, which is all about the struggle to solve, as he puts it in *The Woodlanders*, 'the immortal puzzle – given the man and woman, how to find a basis for their sexual relation' (39). Hardy said that he felt 'very strongly that the position of man and woman in nature may be taken up and treated frankly' (E. Blunden, 1942).

Thomas Hardy is as obsessed with sex as any other novelist, but that's only because his texts reflect his socio-cultural environment; because the Western world, from the Renaissance onwards (some would say from Classic Greek times onwards, or earlier), is obsessed with sexuality. Sex is the norm; anything outside of that is regarded suspiciously. Sue and Jude, and Tess, Grace Melbury and Anne Garland, are pursued for being non-sexual exactly as modern day celebrities who don't seem particularly interested in rutting away are regarded as abnormal by the media. It's the time when questions such as this are asked: *what, you haven't got a lover/ car/ house/ phone/ fax/ computer/ video [insert item as applicable]?* Hardy shows how society polices itself, how it constructs its sexual norms. Hardy would undoubtedly have ventured into gay and lesbian politics, had he been writing in the early 21st century (one wonders how much Hardy would have been sympathetic to, for instance, lesbian feminism, with its talk of femme tops, butch bottoms, femmes butched out, cross-dressing, butch fags in drag, butches 'femmed-out in drag', dildoes, lesbian porn, S/M porn, transvetism, camp and gender-fucking).[18]

The non-sexual activity of the modern celebrity arouses suspicion then often vindictive hassling: the tabloid press ask is s/he gay? perverted? impotent? and so on. As for the idea of friendship, holding hands, dancing, sleeping together, being together, all of this means a sexual relationship is going on: in the media and society, holding hands or doing the things that romantic, sexual couples do is not allowed unless one *is* a romantic, sexual couple[19] In Hardy's novels, if two people hold hands, it is assumed they are in a sexual relationship. Time after time characters hold hands without being in a sexual relationship, then someone sees them. They colour up, they blush, they realize that their every gesture displays to the world their sexual identity. Sometimes it seems that to be sexual at all can be seen as a subversive act, especially outside the 'nuclear family', as American filmmaker Karin Kay noted.[20]

Hardy's women often faint, collapse, blush, go into a fever, all because of love. So important is love to Hardy's characters, that when love's course goes awry, his characters (especially the women) faint, weep or wither away. They literally die for love. And women, being the 'weaker sex', show more signs of decay than men. Hardy's narrators set out to challenge the norms of gender identity, where women are the 'weaker vessel', lapsing into hysteria, but end up submitting to the patriarchal codes.[21] Unable to describe the response to love internally, Hardy's narrators resort, in women, to extraordinary blushes, palpitations, shiverings, sobs and falls. It is one of the most annoying aspects of Hardy's fiction, these sudden blushes or collapses. For example, when Owen recognizes Anne Seaway to be an impostor in *Desperate Remedies*, she colours up like a rainbow: her skin goes ashen grey while her pink cheeks turn purple (18. 1). The insistence on lovers reacting instantly and physically to situations is ridiculous. It is a failure of Hardy's narrators that they can't get inside the characters, but have to show their suffering on the outside. Hardy's women are like painters' canvases or movie screens in this respect, instantly displaying their emotions via uncontrollable tremblings and blushings.

Nature – sexuality, rather – is cruel in Thomas Hardy's fiction. It bypasses delicate education and civilization and careful make-up jobs, erupting in (women's) bodies uncontrollably, showing how they feel, though they might prefer to hide their emotions. Some of Hardy's women react violently to emotional shocks, as if they can't handle them: Viviette shrieks and dies in Swithin's arms in *Two on a Tower*; Miss Aldclyffe bursts a blood vessel and dies after her son's suicide in *Desperate Remedies*; Cytherea, like Grace Melbury, falls ill when it's uncertain about her marital status, and so on.

Underpinning part of *Jude the Obscure* is a utopian vision of a new relation between the sexes. Even the relatively staid Phillotson suggests that single parenthood may be preferrable to the traditional nuclear family: '"I don't see why the woman and the children should not be the unit without the man"'. Gillingham responds: '"[b]y the Lord Harry! – Matriarchy!"' (IV. iv) In their lives Sue and Jude are groping towards such a state, although Sue Bridehead defers to Jude many times, as when she indulges him in his Christminster dream at the Remembrance Day celebrations, even when she knows how destructive it could be. Hardy's text does not go as far as feminist separatism, though, which some feminists, often lesbian feminists, see as 'the centre, the beating heart, the essence'.[22] In lesbian and radical feminist separatism, women keep themselves not only physically but culturally and psychologically apart from men.[23]

Thomas Hardy did not go as far as advocating such an all-female or 'matriarchal' zone, but one can see how sympathetic Hardy was to feminism, and how he would probably embrace if not radical lesbian separatism, then at least the feminist emphasis on *différance* (*pace* Jacques Derrida, Luce Irigaray, Monique Wittig). The search of Sue and Jude for a cultural place where they can love according to rules they have written themselves accords with the quest in radical lesbianism for an extra-patriarchal space. Much of *Jude the Obscure* is about being 'different' – not biologically or sexually, but socially and culturally. Monique Wittig says that the lesbian is crucial because '[l]esbian is the only concept that I know of which is beyond the categories of sex (man and woman)'.[24] Hardy would probably feel sympathetic to the lesbian and feminist quests for a new kind of socio-sexual identity. The difference is that Hardy posits his opposing discourses (Sue and Jude versus society) wholly within patriarchal culture, while radical lesbian feminism aims to go beyond patriarchy. The lesbian may exist outside of traditional heterosexual discourse, but Sue and Jude do not step beyond it. Sue and Jude are locked into two-term masculine logic, where only 'man' or 'woman' exist. All the characters in *Jude the Obscure* adhere to patriarchal constructions, from Gillingham and Phillotson, to Widow Edlin, Arabella, the people of Christminster and the colleges.

The terrible truth for lovers to learn in Thomas Hardy's fiction is that what one loves most can destroy one. The deeper they sink into love, the worse it gets for Hardy's lovers. Yet even when they are treated appallingly by their beloveds, Hardy's lovers love them even more. They 'desperately apotheosise those who reject their love',[25] they dig their own emotional graves, they hurt even more and wallow in it. Hardy's lovers embrace their own destruction.

All Thomas Hardy's lovers dream of a total, all-consuming, and lasting love between two adults. This is part of the sovereignty of 'compulsory heterosexuality', as Adrienne Rich calls it. In her essay on *Romeo and Juliet*, Julia Kristeva writes:

If desire is fickle, thirsting for novelty, unstable by definition, what is it that leads love to dream of an eternal couple? Why faithfulness, the wish for a durable harmony, why in short a marriage of love – not as necessity in a given society but as desire, as libidinal necessity?[26]

The problem is that love and the couple is always a problem, is always fraught with problems. Maybe it's because, as Freud suggests, in the narcissism of love, hatred is deeper and more ancient than love.[27] Certainly in Hardy's fiction, as in most fiction and art, bourgeois romantic love is presented as a struggle, where the lovers are in conflict with the social order (*Jude the Obscure*), with parents and the past (*Tess of the d'Urbervilles*), with neighbours (*The Return of the Native*), with education and background (*The Woodlanders*), and so on. As Cytherea says in *Desperate Remedies*, '"it is difficult to adjust our outer and inner life with perfect harmony to all!"' (13.3). 'As soon as an *other* appears different from myself, it becomes alien, repelled, repugnant, abject – hated' writes Julia Kristeva (1987, 22, also 1982). In Hardy's novels one sees so clearly the simultaneous desire and revulsion – in the love affair of Sue and Jude, for instance, where the œdipal tension is in conflict with the erotic interplay of lovers. Love, for Kristeva, following the Freudian model, is a means of identification and abdication:

Amatory identification, Einfühlung *(the assimilation of other people's feelings), appears to be madness when seen in the light of Freud's caustic lucidity: the ferment of collective hysteria in which crowds abdicate their own judgment, a hypnosis that causes us to lose perception of reality since we hand it over in the* Ego *Ideal. The object in hypnosis devours or absorbs the ego, the voice of consciousness becomes blurred, "in loving blindness one becomes a criminal without remorse"* – the object has taken the place of what was the ego ideal. (1987, 24-25)

Thomas Hardy's notion of love, as expressed in his fiction, is so firmly bound up with notions of art and artifice that one cannot discuss love in Hardy's work without mentioning how it is represented in art. For Hardy, the two modes of experience and ideology, love and art, are inseparable. In Hardy's concept of love, the myth of Narcissus is prominent: that is, the self-reflexivity of love, the *mise-en-âbyme* of love, the auto-eroticism of love, love as a crystallizing mirror in the Stendhalian manner. In Plato's *Symposium*, love is of/ for the other, the other half of one's being. One searches for the completeness to be found in the beloved. The beloved thus becomes that missing fragment which rounds out the desiring self. In Neoplatonism, there is a shift towards a different kind of narcissism. In Plotinus' *Enneads*, love is God, but God is also Narcissus. In Plotinus, the One is 'simultaneously the *loved one* and *love*; He is *love of himself*; for He is beautiful only by and in Himself' (*Enneads*, VI, 8, 15). With Neoplatonism, a new kind of love is born, one founded on interiority and autoeroticism. Narcissus loves himself, he is both subject and object. His real object of desire is an image of himself, that is, representation, art. Julia Kristeva writes:

He loves, he loves Himself – active and passive, subject and object... The object of Narcissus is psychic space; it is representation itself, fantasy. But he does not know it, and he dies. If he knew it he would be an intellectual, a creator of speculative fictions, an artist, writer, psychologist, psychoanalyst. He would be Plotinus or Freud.[28]

The appearance of the lover, especially in late adolescence, can be very disruptive, as Tess Durbeyfield, Jude Fawley, Eustacia Vye and Hardy's other doomed lovers find out. Julia Kristeva offers remarks which apply to the fundamental sense of solitude at the heart of Hardy's fiction – that, after love has been enjoyed, and pain is to be endured, solitude is inevitable:

Erotic fantasy merges with philosophical meditation in order to reach the focus where the sublime and the abject, making up the pedestal of love, come together in the "flash." ...The contemporary narrative (from Joyce to Bataille) has a post-theological aim: to communicate the amorous flash. The one in which the "I" reaches the paranoid dimensions of the sublime divinity while remaining close to abject collapse, disgust with the self. Or, quite simply, to its moderate version know as solitude.[29]

If art comes out of the 'crises of subjectivity',[30] as Kristeva suggests, and any number of artists' work could be cited to support her theory, then melancholy and solitude are inevitable. Melancholy is indeed the natural state of many poets and writers – especially love poets (think of Francesco Petrarch, Bernard de Ventadour, Giraut de Borneil, Emily Brontë, Emily Dickinson, William Shakespeare, Louise Labé, and others). The artist writes of love to bring back love. Metaphor becomes the mechanism by which love is reactivated, metaphor becomes 'the point at which ideal and affect come together in language'.[31] So important is writing and making art for some artists, that they are not really 'alive' unless they are making art. Many is the writer who does not feel a day has been spent well unless it has involved some writing. Writers often speak of feeling uneasy (or guilty) if they have not been writing.

Julia Kristeva's description of Fyodor Dostoievsky, in her study of melancholia, *Black Sun*, has some bearing on Thomas Hardy's fiction. Dostoievsky, Kristeva says, made suffering the keynote of his novels. But it was the 'non-eroticized suffering' of 'primary masochism', that is, melancholy.[32] For Kristeva, Dostoievksian melancholia was 'the primordial psychic inscription of a rupture' (*Black Sun*, 186). Dostoievky's form of suffering is 'neither inside nor outside, between two, at the threshold of the separation self/ other, even before this is possible' (ib.). In Dostoievky's fictional world, which has many affinities with Hardy's fictive world, suffering, voluptuously, is essential; humanity is driven by pain, not pleasure.

Thus far, Kristeva's analysis of Dostoievsky relates directly to Thomas Hardy's art. But Kristeva goes further, suggesting that for Dostoievsky writing produces forgiveness. Dostoievsky, like Hardy, identified deeply with his characters (like all writers do). Dostoievsky thus 'travelled hell' with his characters (James Joyce's phrase), just as Hardy does with Tess or Jude or Henchard. The rebirth of the characters becomes the author's own. Writing is thus an act of signifying suffering which produces forgiveness, or as Kristeva has it, 'between suffering and acting out, æsthetic activity is forgiveness' (*Black Sun*, 200).

One can see how the relations between forgiveness, suffering and writing relate directly to Thomas Hardy's work. But asking forgiveness of whom? The mother, of course. It is the mother, or a mother-substitute, that the writer asks forgiveness of, according to Julia Kristeva. The mother is the one 'who has been killed by signs in the quest for individuality'. Forgiveness, then, is fundamentally equivalent to a reconciliation with the mother. This also fits in with with the view of Hardy as a writer soaked in the mother-world, in the poetic evocation of (lost) maternal spaces.

All of the elements in the above discussion of love and sexual politics in Thomas Hardy's fiction can be seen in his poems, in particular his love poems. The more well-known of the love poems include 'Thoughts of Phena', 'At Rushy Pond', 'Alike and Unlike', 'The Recalcitrants', 'A Second Attempt', 'Rain On a Grave' and 'He Prefers Her Earthly'. Each of the following extracts from Hardy's love poems offer extra dimensions to the erotic relationships in the novels:

> *The eternal tie which binds us twain in one*
> *   No eye will see*
> *Stretching across the miles that sever you and me.*
> ('In Death Divided', SP, 198)

> *When soul in soul reflected,*
> *We breathed an æthereal air.*
> ('Unknowing', CP, 58)

> *...that first look and touch,*
> *Love, doomed us two!*
> ('Last Love-Word', CP, 743)

In the poetry there is a deep sense of self, of the poet's self or persona, as the poetry is composed in the first person: thus: 'I have done all I could | For that lady I knew!' ('The Tree and the Lady', CP, 531), 'Woman much

74

missed, how you call to me' ('The Voice', CP, 346). Hardy speaks of '[h]earts quick as ours in those days' ('A Two-Years' Idyll', CP, 628). 'Love lures life on' he writes in 'Lines' (CP, 458). And in 'After a Journey' he says:

I see what you are doing: you are leading me on
To the spots we know when we haunted here together. (CP, 349)

The rustling of the gown or dress as one of the erotic marks of the woman (in *The Return of the Native*, for example), occurs in 'On a Heath':

I could hear a gown-skirt rustling
Before I could see her shape... (SP, 26)

In *Desperate Remedies* Thomas Hardy's narrator speaks of the acute sensitivity women have in their clothes: when Manston is standing next to Cytherea, she is painfully aware that her clothes are touching his: 'to a woman her dress is part of her body' (8. 4). Here is an early example of the 'hystericization of the body' that one finds in French feminism, where Hélène Cixous and Luce Irigaray speak of the whole of a woman's body being 'sexuate' or sexually sensitive.

The poem 'In a Wood' is sub-titled 'See *The Woodlanders*':

Heart-half and spirit-lame,
City-opprest,
Unto this wood I came
As to a nest;
Dreaming that sylvan peace
Offered the harrowed ease –
Nature a soft release
From man's unrest. (CP, 64)

As the American feminist Camille Paglia put it:

A love poem cannot be simplistically read as a literal, journalistic record of an event or relationship; there is always some fictive reshaping of reality for dramatic or psychological ends. A love poem is secondary rather than primary experience; as an imaginative construction, it invites detached contemplation of the spectacle of sex.[33]

This is why it is foolish of biographers of Thomas Hardy (or any critic) to assume that each poem describes a particular event. Hardy biographers are particularly guilty of claiming that this or that poem must refer to this or that moment in, say, the Hardy-Emma romance in Cornwall.

PART TWO
Feminism in Thomas Hardy's Novels

IV

The Themes of Power, Images and Looking in *Far From the Madding Crowd*

When *Far From the Madding Crowd* appeared (anonymously) in the *Cornhill Magazine,* a critic reckoned that the author was female – was George Eliot. Henry James dryly remarked that Thomas Hardy had studied Eliot well, in order to reproduce the qualities of her rustic characters (1874, in 1957). In *Far From the Madding Crowd* there is but little preamble before the ubiquitous romance between the Hardyan lovers occurs. By the third page Gabriel Oak is gazing erotically at Bathsheba Everdene. This is quite the opposite of, say, *The Return of the Native* or *Jude the Obscure,* where the long-awaited object of desire seems to keep postponing their arrival (as far as the yearning Eustacia and Jude are concerned).

The first four chapters of *Far From the Madding Crowd* are like a mini-Hardy romantic drama, with a brief courtship, proposal, rejection and disillusion. It has many of the classic Hardyan motifs: the woman on horseback or a cart, the man standing (like the 'La Belle Dame Sans

Merci' sequence in *A Pair of Blue Eyes*), the class difference (the 'poor man and the lady' scenario), the erotic spying, and the imagery of psychological barriers (Oak and Bathsheba talk over hedges or rosebushes). The reader knows Oak's sudden marriage proposal won't work – this is the beginning of a medium-sized romantic novel, with marriage expected at the end. Plus it's a Hardy novel, which means weddings = funerals. Oak proposes after meeting Bathsheba only once or twice. His lack of knowledge of women and sexual relations is demonstrated by his idea that a sophisticated person like Bathsheba would be satisfied with a 'nice snug little farm' and him (IV).

Frank Troy is usually seen as the phallic one, gazing at (and thereby controlling) Bathsheba; but there are moments when Troy feminizes himself, or is feminized – as when he puts on the bee-hiver's clothes, or when he dresses up as a circus performer (L. Shires, 54). His identity is not as thoroughly masculine as it at first appears: he feels constricted as the 'Professor of Gymnastics, Pugilism, Sword Exercises, Roughriding'. Hardy's narrator makes it clear that Troy's sword display corresponds to sexual intercourse; as in pornography, the narrator concentrates on Bathsheba's bodily responses to Troy's phallic thrusts. Afterwards, Bathsheba feels she has 'sinned a great sin'. The 'sin' here refers to a kiss, but it's obvious it means much more than that.

Long before the famous phallic sword-wielding scene between Troy and Bathsheba, there are easily spotted erotic moments in the narrative, such as the frequent scenes surrounding sheep: Oak sticking the lance into the sheep when they're blasted; Oak sharpening his shears with Bathsheba; Oak shearing the ewe while Bathsheba looks on. These are all fairly standard scenes that stand in for sexual acts. For example, in the shears-sharpening scene, both participants simulate tupping, turning the handle, going up and down, while the other one does the sharpening. You don't need to be an expert in Sigmund Freud's psychoanalysis or Elizabethan bawdy to see what's happening here. Unable to show sex, Hardy simply has some other scene stand in for it, with Gabriel sharpening his 'tool'.

It occurs again in the Great Barn, when Oak throws a ewe over his shoulder, turning her this way and that, again pretty direct simulations of tupping. Bathsheba's observing him, and notes how the ewe '"blushes at the insult"' of being shorn (XXII). To ram home the point (so to speak), later on in the scene when Boldwood appears to steal and ride off with Bathsheba, Oak's sexual jealousy causes him to harm the sheep – in the groin, of course. Oak's piercing the sheep neatly demonstrates his erotic envy, as well as what he'd like to do to Boldwood. There are also suggestions of Freudian castration here, and the links between Lacanian looking and castration (the pleasure of voyeurism may lead to castration). The ewe may also be an emblem for Gabriel's femininity, one critic suggests, so that wounding the ewe is an act of 'symbolic self-castration, to avoid being more deeply wounded' (L. Shires, 58).

The relation between looking and longing in *Far From the Madding Crowd* became one of Thomas Hardy's perennial themes. By the time of *Jude the Obscure* in 1895 it had reached its fullest and most subtle expression. Jude Fawley gazing lingeringly at Sue Bridehead is a summary of all of the love affairs in Hardy's fiction, from *Under the Greenwood Tree* to *The Well-Beloved*. Jude gazes voyeuristically, in the classic Lacanian optical eroticization of the obscure object of desire, where the eye is a 'kind of phallus' (see J. Zipes, 1986, 258; L. Mykyta, 1983). In the Lacanian system of scopophilia, as post-Lacanian feminists have pointed out, male, phallic desire is affirmed, and sustained (see M. Humm, 1989, 84; L. Gamman, 1988; L. Mulvey, 1989). In Hardy's fiction, as in most love poetry and romantic fiction, it (love) is all done with the eyes and looks. Lacanians would say love (erotic desire) is all done with mirrors, narcisstically reflecting each other.

Just as Dante's *dolce stil novo* verse or the troubadours' poetry was essentially a literary tradition,[1] so Sue and Jude's erotic relationship is highly literary and verbal. They talk about love more than doing it. They perform it, analyze it, deconstruct it, seldom indulging in anything as demonstratively physical as a kiss.[2]

Bathsheba Everdene is a character given a superficial treatment by the narrator, who does not bother at times to cloak his sexism:

Bathsheba, though she had too much understanding to be entirely governed by her womanliness, had too much womanliness to use her understanding to the best advantage. (166)

The narrator of *Far From the Madding Crowd*, as in most of Hardy's novels, cannot resist putting down the female characters in many subtle and some not-so-subtle ways. The narrator has Bathsheba admit often to her own 'weakness' compared to men. Bathsheba tells Troy: '"I am not a fool, although I am a woman, and have my woman's moments"' (XLI). When, in the gentle form of sisterhood or female companionship that Bathsheba enjoys (with Liddy and the other servants), Liddy tells her she appears as threatening as men (XXX). Bathsheba is taken aback by this image of her as an Amazon – she deflates the idea, hoping that she is not '"a bold sort of maid – mannish"'.

Sue Bridehead's thoughts on women being viewed by patriarchy as 'property', and on the inadequacy of masculine language to describe feminine experience, are already present in Thomas Hardy's fiction in Bathsheba's comments, such as '"I *hate* to be thought men's property in that way"' (IV). Bathseba Everdene also says, in a statement that looks forward directly to feminism's reappraisals of 'male-made language' (Dale Spender, Kate Millett, Elaine Showalter *et al*), '"[i]t is difficult for a woman to define her feelings in language which is chiefly made by men to express theirs"' (LI).

Male critics have exalted Gabriel Oak as the stalwart lover who wins his reward (Bathsheba) for such diligent, apparently selfless labouring. Feminist critics have noted how Gabriel is feminized – how he exhibits the traits the Victorian era attributed to women (passivity, tenderness, humility, patience). Even the name Gabriel connotes androgynous creatures, angels, who had as many, if not more feminine attributes than masculine ones (look at Pre-Raphaelite paintings contemporary with *Far From the Madding Crowd*, for example). Also, Gabriel acts like Tess at times, and like other female and feminized male characters: he falls asleep or is passive at crises (he is also the only 'true man' at other crisis points, such as when he saves the hay ricks when every other male is drunk or asleep).

It is partly Bathsheba's 'light-weight' personality, in comparison to other Thomas Hardy heroines, that makes *Far From the Madding Crowd* seem one of Hardy's 'minor' novels. It is usually put in with the 'major' novels, but is not seen by mainstream Hardy criticism as one of the 'tragic novels'. There are 'tragic' elements in the novel: there are three deaths – Fanny's, Troy's, and Boldwood's 'suicide', giving himself up for one of Hardy's 'living deaths'.

Far From the Madding Crowd is in many ways the archetypal Thomas Hardy novel: it depicts one woman being courted by three men from various classes, interspersed with events from the agricultural year and a set of gnarled rustic characters. Sargeant Troy is the prototype of later phallic seducers, such as Fitzpiers and Alec d'Urberville; Oak is the typical Hardyan lover, quiet but ardent, the prototype for Giles, Clym and Jude.

In these and many other ways *Far From the Madding Crowd* lays the foundations for much of Thomas Hardy's subsequent fiction. Class, for example, is a key element of the erotic attachments between Fanny and Troy, Oak and Bathsheba, and so on. One would think, in a way, that Boldwood was the ideal Hardyan lover: he is quiet, self-contained, and tremendously passionate. In the chapter where he pours out his heart to Bathsheba – XXXI, "Blame – Fury" – Boldwood comes across as possessing most of the qualities the ideal Hardyan lover ought to have: total subservience to the beloved; belief in love; the promise of (and visible means of offering) material security; nobility; pride; education, and so on. At first, apart from the age difference, it is not certain what is exactly wrong with Boldwood – not so much from Bathsheba's point of view, but from the narrator's and the reader's. As far as the typical Hardy novel is concerned, Boldwood appears quite worthy as a potential lover (he doesn't enhance his love-suit, however, by telling Bathsheba '"[y]ou wouldn't let a dog suffer what I have suffered, could you but know it!"' LIII). Later, the narrator delineates some of Boldwood's faults. Among them is his over-bearing emotion: '[h]is equilibrium disturbed, he was in extremity at once. If an emotion possessed him at all, it ruled him' (XVIII). Again, it seems as if Boldwood has the required Hardyan erotic intensity: emotionally, he goes all the way, he is all or nothing. But no, it's not enough: the narrator adds that there was no lightness or subtlety in Boldwood's emotions. Later, as Boldwood is preparing for the fateful Christmas party, he confesses to Oak that he is blithe and 'more than cheerful', but he also fears happy moods, because trouble seems not far away (LII). Boldwood is one of those curious Hardyan characters whose basic disposition is melancholy, who fear moods such as happiness because it disrupts their lives (Tess is also like this).

Boldwood is in love not so much with Bathsheba herself, but with his imagined version of her, a figment, adored from a distance. 'Boldwood worships his own ability to look, his own sexual urge, and his own imagined objectification' (L. Shires, 55). As soon as Boldwood meets Bathsheba for real, in the flesh and blood, his fantasized projections of her conflict greatly with the real woman. Boldwood makes great plans for their future life together, imagining himself with her, but every time he meets her, these mental edifices are destroyed.

The dialogue between Frank Troy and Bathsheba Everdene when they meet at night in the woods and her dress is caught on him is ridiculous.

> *"We have got hitched together somehow, I think."*
> *"Yes."*
> *"Are you a woman."*
> *"Yes."*
> *"A lady, I should have said."*
> *"It doesn't matter."*
> *"I am a man."*
> *"Oh!"* (XXIV)

Ignoring the fact that it would idiotic for Troy to say '"I am a man"', which would have been patently obvious to Bathsheba from the three sentences he has already spoken, what stands out is the narrator orchestrating the dialogue to get straight to the heart of the theme of the novel: sexual relations. Thus, Troy says he is a man and asks Bathsheba if she is a woman. The (heterosexual) erotic relationship between Bathsheba and Troy is immediately set in motion, then. It is the man, too, who determines the pattern of the representation, by confirming that she is a woman and he is a man. His sexual conquest of her, if he voiced it, would be made along these lines to an outsider: 'she's a woman, and I'm a man'. That bare fact of their gender justifies everything that follows, as far as the ideology of the novel (and the era) is concerned. The rest of the narration on Troy bolsters his simple sexism. The way he treats and views women, tries to keep them in place, it all stems from this view that he is a man, and she (whoever she is) is a woman.

Fanny's death halfway through the novel indicates that the narrative is not going to be a simple, lightweight pastoral romance. The scene with the open coffin also indicates the depth of the narrative – far deeper than soap opera or melodrama. Fanny's ironic position is that she is more eloquent when she is dead. Alive, she is absent for much of the narrative. Her presence is at first shadowy: she is first seen as a blur addressing a wall at night; then she is seen by Gabriel again at night. Dead, though, she becomes supremely, vengefully visible and voluble.

As a corpse, Fanny becomes very active, her presence cannot be erased; she enacts her 'revenge' – not only on Troy, as physical evidence of his messy past, but also on society, on the patriarchal system (J. Kincaid, 140). It is partly Thomas Hardy's love of the macabre that enables him to set the confrontation between wife, husband and lover beside an open coffin at night. The meetings and admissions of desire and betrayal could have occurred on the road to Casterbridge. Troy recognizes Fanny's voice, but keeps his back turned to her. There could easily have been a passionate confrontation here, with Fanny begging Troy to help her, and Troy eventually admitting to his duplicity. The dead baby adds an extra *frisson* to the coffin scene. It's another manifestation of one of Hardy's most abiding themes: sex and children before marriage ('"[a]ll romances end at marriage"' says Troy to Bathsheba, XLI).

The narrator of *Far From the Madding Crowd* milks Fanny's death for it's worth. Not content with having her die and all Troy's adultery being exposed, Hardy's narrator has first the coffin scene, then the churchyard and gargoyle sequence. While the open coffin scene may be familiar from Gothic and horror novels, the gargoyle seems to be an example of Hardy's original imagination. It brings together the familiar Hardyan themes – of 'too late beloved' (love coming too late); the death of the beloved; churchyards and graves; love as a funeral ('weddings be funerals'); and the peculiarities of ecclesiastical architecture.

The quirk of the churchyard scene is Thomas Hardy's eye for religious architecture, the way a gargoyle can point in a particular direction and gush during heavy rains. This is one of the first really powerful instances in Hardy's fiction of his fierce critique of Christianity. It is a bizarre sequence, when the rain pours on the grave and turns all the flowers (beauty) to mud (death). Here Hardy expresses his aggressive suspicion of religious structures – yet the narrator is partially excused from being anti-Christian by having the 'cause' of the desecration a 'natural' force, rain. It is not the church building itself that harms Fanny's grave, but rain. Of course, it is the peculiarities of church architecture that shapes and directs the natural forces. Christianity cannot save people from the severity of nature when it wishes to be violent. People may try to shelter under Christianity, but it won't protect them totally: Troy shelters under the church and has a 'comfortless sleep'; Fanny, dead, is also not 'comforted' by Christianity, which indirectly desecrates her grave.

Even at this early stage in Thomas Hardy's career as a writer, his doubts about the comforts of religion are deep. Yet what counts for Troy is going through the ritual of buying the grave stone and the flowers. Turning away from Fanny in life, he, oddly, lavishes attention on her in death. The irony of his belated acts is what antagonizes him when he sees the ruined grave. Again, it is 'too little, too late', as with many of Hardy's narratives. Troy's lavish treatment of Fanny in death is itself an oddity, a 'remorseful reaction from previous indifference' (XLV). His lack of drive at this low point is vividly indicated when Hardy's narrator has him simply make his way south, without hardly considering his wife or life behind him, and going to Lulwind Cove for a swim. The ritual elements of this act, to wash away his sins and crimes, are obvious. There is also the desire to lose himself in the utter immensity of the ocean, to forget himself and his individuality. When Bathsheba hides in the ferny hollow, which recalls Tess crawling into the wood, the comparison with a womb and rebirth is obvious. It is as if both Bathsheba and Tess have to start again, from this rebirth. To indicate the lowness of Bathsheba's life at this point, the next day she finds that the hollow was not protective at all, but full of pestilent growths.

The emphasis on the first, religious marriage in *Jude the Obscure*, which Sue Bridehead regards as truer than her second 'marriage' with Jude Fawley, is echoed in *Far From the Madding Crowd*. At the crucial coffin scene, when Bathseba Everdene confronts Troy with his betrayal, he says that he is more 'morally' Fanny's than hers. Bathsheba is horrified, and emits 'a long low cry of measureless despair and indignation, such a wail of anguish as had never before been heard within those old-inhabited walls' (XLIII). Oddly pious all of a sudden, Troy addresses the dead Fanny Robin: '"in the sight of Heaven you are my very, very wife!"' Sue uses exactly the same terms to justify the significance of her marriage with Phillotson in *Jude the Obscure*. The recourse of Sue to Christianity is understandable, but in Troy it's bizarre. Troy asks Bathsheba when they first meet: '"are you a woman?"' The answer the text gives is that Fanny is 'more' of a woman than Bathsheba. Fanny has at least given Troy a child, one of the marks of 'womanhood' for patriarchal society.

Thomas Hardy's feminism in *Far From the Madding Crowd* is mild compared to the stridency of, say, *Jude the Obscure*. What's noteworthy is that Bathsheba Everdene is so young, like Tess Durbeyfield, by the end of the novel (she's only 24). Yet she has endured much: journeyed through three love affairs, much emotional complexity, the shooting of one lover, and another lover becoming a murderer. Like *Under the Greenwood Tree*, *Far From the Madding Crowd* ends with what ought to be a happy occasion, a wedding. The ending of *Under the Greenwood Tree* hinted that the lovers would not have a wholly smooth time of it. In *Far From the Madding Crowd* the wedding is not a joyous finale to a fairy tale. The narrator suggests the changes in Bathsheba in phrases such as '[t]hen Oak laughed, and Bathsheba smiled (for she never laughed readily now)' (LVII).

In *Far From the Madding Crowd* Thomas Hardy's narrator does not overtly question the dominant sexual politics of the time. Rather, the narrator often weights his discourse in favour of masculine ideology, as is apparent from the many sexist remarks the narrator makes. What occurs with *Far From the Madding Crowd*, though, that does not happen with the same intensity in Hardy's earlier fiction (such as *Under the Greenwood Tree* and *Desperate Remedies*), is the exploration of the ways in which humans are vile to each other, either unconsciously or not, as manifested primarily in sexual and economic relationships. The penultimate paragraph of *Far From the Madding Crowd*, though, hints at a different kind of marriage – that of 'good-fellowship – *camaraderie*' (LVI). Not a marriage of erotic romance but a working together, a common labour which, the narrator suggests, 'proves itself to be the only love which is as strong as death'. However, this new friendship-based marriage is celebrated by a host of men, a mass of noise, a cannon firing, and Oak getting used to calling Bathsheba 'wife'.

V

'To Be Loved to Madness': Eustacia Vye and *The Return of the Native*

Eustacia Vye receives a really enthusiastic introduction and description from the narrator of *The Return of the Native*. No other Thomas Hardy character has received such a star-billing as Eustacia Vye. Tess Durbeyfield is loved by her narrator, clearly, and receives much exalted prose. But Eustacia has the full force of Hardy's poetry washed over her. William Shakespeare's description of Cleopatra is particularly feverish, but the throne speech, for instance, is mediated through an onlooker. In *Antony and Cleopatra*, as in *Romeo and Juliet* or *Love's Labour's Lost*, the passionate glorifications of the beloved are done through a character. In *The Return of the Native*, there is no character, except perhaps Clym, who could come close to speaking the 'high art' poetry of the "Queen of Night" chapter. Only sophisticated characters such as Angel can conjure up names of Goddesses when they praise their beloveds. Angel likens Tess to Artemis and Demeter. She, in her direct way, retorts '"[c]all me Tess"' (XX).

Eustacia Vye is described as nothing less than a Goddess, which is the highest form of exaltation that occurs in the Western (patriarchal) world. It is worth quoting from some of the "Queen of Night" chapter in *The Return of the Native*, to illustrate just how gushing Hardy's evocation of Eustacia is:

> *She had the passions and instincts which make a model goddess... She had Pagan eyes, full of nocturnal mysteries... The mouth, seemed formed less to speak than to quiver, less to quiver than to kiss... Her presence brought memories of such things as Bourbon roses, rubies, and tropical midnights; her moods recalled lotus-eaters and the march in 'Athalie'; her motions, the ebbs and flow of the sea; her voice, the viola.... Her appearance accorded well with this smouldering rebelliousness, and the shady splendour of her beauty was the real surface of the sad and stifled warmth within her. A true Tartarean dignity sat upon her brow... (I. vii)*

Thomas Hardy throws all he's got into the description of Eustacia. He raids the pantheon of former poets to gather apt allusions – to Goddesses such as Athena, Hera and Artemis; at the same time as the narrator exalts Eustacia Vye as a Goddess, he remarks that she is no 'model woman' (I. vii). This is Eustacia's problem: she is too extraordinary for Egdon Heath, as every character notes. The rustic chorus – Timothy Fairway, Grandfer Cantle, Sam, Humphrey, Christian – all regard Eustacia as something special, someone who does not fit into the Egdon scheme of things.

The portrait of Eustacia Vye, once regarded as an example of 'great description', is now seen by (masculinist) criticism as overblown.[1] 'Eustacia Vye,' writes Leonard Deen, 'more than any other of Hardy's protagonists, seems intended to be grandly heroic' (1960, 207). Robert Heilman presents a typical masculinist view:

> *What she [Eustacia] cannot sustain – as who could? – are the implied comparisons with Clotho, Lachesis, and Atorpos, with Artemis, Athena, and Hera, with Héloïse and Cleopatra. (1979, 65)*

For some critics, Thomas Hardy's attempts to mythicize Eustacia Vye and make her a 'tragic' figure fail (R. Evans, 257; R. Heilman, 1979, 84; I. Gregor, 1974, 85f; L. Deen, 208). Hardy's narrator is ambivalent about Eustacia's greatness (or his literary exaltation of her), for she is also seen as 'comically pretentious' (D. Eggenchwiler, 448f). The idea is that male/masculinist critics do not see Eustacia's character living up to the mythical allusions of the narrator. It's because, perhaps, the description of Eustacia breaks the naturalistic narration of the rest of the novel. For critics, it's OK for Shakespeare to describe Cleopatra in a rich (and rightly famous) passage, but not for Hardy to go overboard with his depiction of a young provincial woman in relatively obscure 19th century Britain.

For another male critic, Lance St John Butler, Eustacia Vye is '[t]oo passionate for her own good... she is at once our tragic goddess and a trapped bird' (L. Butler, 1978, 46). For Butler, the lengthy description of Eustacia is 'both a failure and a success' (ib., 44). Robert Rehder says that Eustacia 'has no inner strength', an astonishing claim, really, for Eustacia is one of Hardy's strongest characters, male or female. Rehder also writes that Eustacia 'is overpowered by the chaos of her feelings. Her emotions destroy her.'[2] These are extraordinary claims, for, surely, it's very much Eustacia's *situation* that destroys her, as much as her feelings. Though she is a suicidal/ tragic character at times, she is really in the wrong place at the right time. This is so often Hardy's way. Wrong place, right time; or right place, wrong time. Tess Durbeyfield, after all, is ready for a tender, affectionate, considerate love when she goes to Alec d'Urberville's house and meets Alec instead of Angel Clare. *Tess*'s narrator remarks that it's a pity that Tess did not meet Angel earlier. This might not have been successful either, for Angel shows himself to be markedly more immature than Tess: if Angel had met Tess at age 16, as she was at the beginning of the novel, he would probably have still have made a mess of their relationship. Tess, though, would have been able to extricate herself from his clutches relatively easily, much easier than it was to deal with Angel years later, as with Alec.

John Peck sees Eustacia Vye as an outsider figure, someone who 'will never really fit in with society' (1987, 87). When Julia Kristeva speaks of the poet, but one can insert witch, or shaman, or outsider; sometimes she uses the term 'hysteric' (A. Jones, 1986, 363). For Kristeva, as 'hysterics' or 'outsiders', the semiotic style of women as writers is likely to involve 'repetitive, spasmodic separations from the dominating discourse, which, more often, they are forced to imitate' (A. Jones, ib.). It's not difficult to see how female characters such as Eustacia and Tess have to imitate the dominant (patriarchal) discourse in order to survive.

The male/ masculinist/ patriarchal form of criticism sees Eustacia Vye as a character overblown by the narrator, given too much æsthetic, mythic and symbolic weight, which she cannot support or carry off. While Michael Henchard happily assumes the proportions of King Lear, Eustacia Vye is not allowed by critics to be (like) Cleopatra or Artemis. It's a critical double standard, where it's OK for male characters to have the mythic treatment, but not for female ones. (This double standard does not operate exclusively on gender lines, for Clym is compared by the authorial voice to John the Baptist, but some critics think he is not fitted to the comparison). Clym and the Baptist, and both Eustacia and Clym being likened to the apostle Paul (R. Heilman, 1979, 82), are improbable allusions, in each case vastly inflated, as with most of the "Queen of the Night" sequence. Eustacia is marginalized by society spatially – she lives a little apart from the rest of the Egdon inhabitants. And when Eustacia and Clym are married they live in isolation from the community (P. Boumelha, 1982, 53).

Desire is the keynote of *The Return of the Native*. It is the pressure of this desire upon the characters that raises *The Return of the Native* up from being merely a series of melodramatic events to something of a tragedy. *The Return of the Native* was clearly intended to be a tragedy in a grand manner, complete with multiple colourful deaths – Wildeve, Mrs Yeobright and Eustacia – and a Gloucester-like blinding of Clym.

The desire in *The Return of the Native* is of course erotic, bourgeois, heterosexual desire, that desire which to be completely fulfilled must be rounded off with marriage. One knows this particular Thomas Hardy novel will not end up happily, because it starts with a failed wedding day. From that botched marriage the waves of desire and frustration fan outwards over the web of social connections on the Heath. From the opening chapters, *The Return of the Native* is the story of people desiring erotic love, or something greater: Charley yearns to touch Eustacia's hand; Eustacia yearns for Wildeve, Clym, Budmouth and Paris, anything; Venn yearns for Thomasin; Clym yearns for his plans, then for Eustacia; Wildeve yearns for Thomasin, Eustacia and something greater. Wildeve is simply the object that Eustacia's erotic yearning alights on. The narrator describes Eustacia's erotic gaze 'twining and untwining about him as the single object within her horizon on which dreams might crystallize' (I. x)

Wildeve is thus interchangeable – with Clym, Budmouth, and Paris. What's important for Eustacia is not Wildeve himself, but her desire. His function is merely to be a pretext for her erotic imaginings, like Beatrice Portinari with Dante Alighieri or the youth for William Shakespeare's poet in the *Sonnets*. What the narrator says of Wildeve could be applied to all of Hardy's lovers: '[t]o be yearning for the difficult, to be weary of that offered; to care for the remote, to dislike the near' (III. vi). Eustacia tells herself '"want of an object to live for – that's all is matter with me!"' (II. iv). When Clym is talked about before his arrival it only requires a few words overhead by Eustacia from the furze-gatherers to furnish her with 'visions enough to fill the whole blank afternoon' (II. i). So susceptible is Eustacia that Clym coming from Paris was 'like a man coming from heaven' (II. i). The last words that Eustacia speaks in *The Return of the Native* – moaning to herself as she traverses rain-dark Egdon Heath, go straight to the theme of the novel: erotic fascination, and the problems it creates. Eustacia says '"[Wildeve's] not *great* enough for me to give myself to – he does not suffice for my desire!"' (V. vii) This is ever Eustacia's problem: that there is, finally, no one 'great' enough for her, and no experience rich enough for her. Like Tess, Eustacia at this moment of desperation imagines her future, the next year dragging on, and the one after that. The vision of a future as intolerable as the present is partly what encourages Eustacia, as with Tess, to end it all. Eustacia's speech ends with 'a frenzy of bitter revolt': '"I do not deserve my lot!"' and she rails against the cruel world ('"the cruelty of putting me into this ill-conceived world!"'). Eustacia's last speech is a form of the suicide's cliché farewell: 'goodbye, cruel world!' As with Tess, the individual just before her end is set against the cruelty of the world, and heaven. Just as Eustacia says she has '"done no harm to Heaven at all!"', so Tess speaks of God and sacrifice at Stonehenge, and Tess's death is set in the religious framework of the gods.

Lacking the ability to say "screw you all" and leave Egdon Heath,

Eustacia Vye Vye is trapped. She can't simply walk to Budmouth and get on a ship. No. She has to stay and fret and fever. Pity. Pity she can't tell the lot of 'em to go to hell, and then get on with her life. It is so sad that she relies on Clym Yeobright to 'save' her. And what a wimp he is when he finally turns up! With his grandiose schemes for educating the natives, he's an 1880s version of the 'New Man' of the 1990s. And Eustacia, as one of the 'New Women' of the late 19th century, is bound to be disappointed. So Eustacia relies on men, and they fail her. Tess relies on Angel, Alec, Angel's father, her father, the vicar, Farmer Groby, and they all fail her. Only certain women help her: Marian, and her mother.

It is wrong for Eustacia Vye to rely on men to deliver her from evil, to remedy her situation, to satisfy her yearning. Because men cannot satisfy such things. They have their own problems, and, as soon as Clym returns, he is beset by his difficulties in realizing his dream of preaching to the masses. They limit each other, Clym and Eustacia. For Eustacia, at the beginning, all seems yearning and ambition, with plans/ hopes for Paris and glamour. Instead of the expected leaps into the turmoil of life, there is only the staid village life on Egdon. As John Goode puts it, for Eustacia there is 'the *double cross* of the heath and her hero's *return*, which both say no' (1988, 40).

It is worse for the women, though. The men have jobs. Their work offers them independence. Thus, Thomasin has no identity in the book unless she is seen in relation to Damon Wildeve or Diggory Venn. Eustacia has some narrational independence – she stalks the Heath alone, and is thus one of those few women in Hardy's fiction who move beyond the boundaries defined by men. Bathsheba Everdene is always defined by the men around her, but Eustacia, like Tess, steps outside of these definitions.

Unfortunately, Eustacia Vye lacks that final decisiveness to get moving. So many of Thomas Hardy's protagonists have the requisite amount of desire – they are full of desire. But they lack that final energy to get them moving. It is the same with Jude Fawley, or Giles Winterbourne, or Tess Durbeyfield. These characters move, but they lack the final effort/ energy/ ability to round off their lives, to make that act of ontological completion. They stop short. Somehow, they fall short of the final mark, which is the attainment of full beingness, or consummation, or total realization, whatever one calls it.

Seeing themselves as commodities to be traded between men, which is a hideous state of affairs, Thomas Hardy's female characters relinquish power in their lives. Thus Eustacia is free to roam the nothingness of the Heath, but she can't go further, she can't go eight miles down the road to the town of Budmouth, to live the life she wants there, or to go on a ship elsewhere.

Eustacia is in a trap, but so is Clym. He is made a victim by his education. For education or learning is usually problematic in Hardy's fiction. The ones who have knowledge are no happier than the ones who don't have it. Education has disrupted Eustacia's equilibrium, says Humphrey, one of the captain's cronies; her father replies that if she had "'less romantic nonsense in her head it would be better for her'" (II. i).

In *The Return of the Native* there is a view of graffiti as vandalism that arises from Thomas Hardy's suspicion of education: if the local youths hadn't learnt to write, they couldn't deface the countryside with 'bad words' (II. i). Here, the older rustic generation lament education because it leads to vandals defacing the landscape with words that shame people. Education usually means progress, but not in Hardy's world. It's all very well to get educated, he says, but it usually doesn't do any good. It creates problems. It creates desires. It shows one that things can be even better, and so there is an even greater gulf between one's ideals and one's actual situation.

Boredom and lassitude lie behind Eustacia's disposition, which is 'modern', in tune with the outsider anti-heroes in the work of Albert Camus, Knut Hamsun, André Gide, Jean-Paul Sartre, John Copwer Powys, Hector Barbusse, J.-K. Huysmans, D.H. Lawrence and Aldous Huxley. The expression of her weariness is typically Gothic-Romantic – '[s]he is a romantic (she is a whole history of romanticism) seen romantically' writes Leonard W. Deen (1960, 211).

Eustacia is introduced as a thoroughly Romanticized personality – in the MS Byron is her 'chief priest' (J. Paterson, 1960, 82). When Eustacia is all desire, she is wonderful, for one feels she is capable of wild deeds, of reaching the female 'wild zone'. True tragedy pivots on the feeling that something extraordinary – terrifying, strange, mystical, dangerous –

might happen at any moment. With Eustacia one feels this. Not with any of the other characters. One feels this wakefulness, this anticipation, with Henchard, Jude, Sue and Tess, but not with any of Hardy's other characters. The others are predictable. But those few tragic characters, they are capable, one feels, of doing amazing things. They have potential, they have life, they can perhaps overturn the humdrum reality of everyday life.

When Eustacia Vye arrives at the Yuletide party in *The Return of the Native*, she knows that '[t]o dance with a man is to concentrate a twelvemonth's regulation fire upon him in the fragment of an hour' (II. v). And this is the whole of Thomas Hardy's narratives, encapsulated here by Eustacia: this concentration of the bliss of love into a few minutes, an hour or so, followed by days, weeks, months and years of vacuum, lack, nostalgia, weeping, longing and memories. This is the whole of Thomas Hardy's fiction, right here, in this thought of Eustacia's. And it is the same thought of Tess, Angel, Jude, Sue, Giles, Grace, Bathsheba, Viviette, Lucetta, Oak, Fancy, Marty, Pierston and Venn.

Once there was bliss and love, and now, for years, there has been no bliss or love. This is all of Thomas Hardy's thought, summed up. Hardy's fiction is reducible to desire, pure desire, always frustrated, never satisfied; and, if satisfied, then only for a moment, an hour or two, then years of lack, loss, lament, lassitude. As D.H. Lawrence writes in *Study of Thomas Hardy*: 'most obviously, from the Wessex novels, the first and chiefest factor is the struggle into love and the struggle with love... The via media to being for man or woman, is love, and love alone' (20).

And this is the problem, this hopeful clinging onto love as the means of coming into being, or achieving self-realization, or solving all one's problems. It's wrong. There are other ways of achieving beingness apart from love. There are all kinds of creative ways of being. But Hardy's characters are limited by their economic-socio-cultural environments. And when some of them get educated, that doesn't help either, because they are taught the wrong things, as children are still taught the wrong things in schools today.

Thomas Hardy's characters yearn so painfully – Eustacia cries out for a great love to help her escape. Her prayer, sent out into the wild heath, is '"[o] deliver my heart from this fearful gloom and loneliness: send me great love from somewhere, else I shall die"' (I. vii). Love, the erotic, narcissistic impulse, proves to be her downfall. She dies for love, like Cathy in *Wuthering Heights*. Hardy's women yearn, but rarely do they get an earthlover like Heathcliff. Intense love means intense death. Love now but die later – this is the Romantic credo. The love between Clym and his mother is equally intense, and destructive. It reaches a profundity of painfulness (III. iii).

Eustacia Vye is confident and clear enough to know what she wants: '[t]o be loved to madness – such was her great desire' (I. vii). And better, Eustacia thinks, that love should blaze then expire, rather than merely glimmer for years. At first, her desire is vague – she loves love more than any particular lover. When Clym returns, she focuses on him. Nothing will do for Eustacia, nor for Sue Bridehead – nothing but absolute transcendence in all matters, nothing but complete fulfilment. When she renews her yearning for Damon Wildeve, early on in the narrative, she focuses her desire upon him out of jealousy, because of the erotic triangle entanglements between her, Thomasin and Wildeve (I. xi). But, a few pages and a few days later, she realizes how mediocre Wildeve actually is, but admitting this to herself means admitting her own faults:

> She was immediately angry at having betrayed even to herself the possible evanescence of her passion for him. She could not admit at once that she might have over-estimated Wildeve, for to perceive his mediocrity now was to admit her own great folly heretofore. (I. xi)

The seeds of the tragedy are in Eustacia's character, as in Thomas Hardy's other tragedies, as in tragic figures such as Othello, Macbeth and Oedipus. But, by extension, one can also say that the seeds of tragedy are also in education, in religion, in society itself, for people are social beings, as Simone de Beauvoir says: and for many feminists, notions of 'the feminine', 'femininity', 'masculinity' and the 'superiority' of men are mostly the result of socialization, of enculturation and education.[3]

So it is Eustacia's character in *The Return of the Native* that creates the tragedy – because she desires something from men that they cannot provide – yet it is what formed Eustacia's character that is also the cause of the tragedy. What made Eustacia Vye? What makes people? Parents and families and schools and people – but, beyond them, social systems, institutions, ideas, habits, dogmas, philosophies – all those things that are more than people, more than individuals. There is no one to 'blame', because one can't 'blame' society, because society is people – it's us. It is no one's 'fault' because it is everybody's fault. But, as revolutions down the ages have shown, it's no use targeting individuals, or even masses of people. Things such as 'society' and 'culture' are greater even than people, even though they are made up of people. And 'society' and 'culture' are only great big abstract terms for things that influence us, that make us. They are at once abstractly intangible, and violently palpable.

So Eustacia Vye's tragedy, like the tragedy of Tess Durbeyfield or Hamlet or Oedipus, is also society's tragedy. And *there's* the rub. Eustacia Vye creates her own demise, but society does too. And all this is clearly marked out when Clym Yeobright arrives and Eustacia focuses her yearning upon him. The dream begins here, but the reality can never live up to it, because it is the wrong sort of dream. Yet Eustacia can't help herself. She goes for the dream:

> *The perfervid woman was by this time half in love with a vision. The fantastic nature of her passion, which lowered her as an intellect, raised her as a soul. If she had a little more self-control she would have attenuated the emotion to nothing by sheer reasoning, and so have killed it off.* (II. iii)

Eustacia knows she wants some kind of satisfaction or completion, but the means are hazy. When love comes along, she digs her talons into it, because it seems to provide a little glamour and excitement in the midst of her dreary provincial world. As D.H. Lawrence writes: '[w]hat does she want? She does not know, but it is evidently some form of self-realisation; she wants to be herself, to attain herself' (*Study*, 23).

Eustacia Vye hasn't as much burning tragedy about her as her forebear, Cathy Earnshaw in *Wuthering Heights*, but Eustacia still burns. Wildeve, unfortunately, is no Heathcliff, despite his name. As the narrator says, voicing Eustacia's thoughts: '[w]hat was Wildeve? Interesting, but inadequate' (II. v). Eustacia is a rather stereotypical romantic heroine. Alternatively, one might see her as a bored teenager stuck in the provinces, like millions of others. She desires glamour, which is a craving socialized into people from an early age, and these days catered for by TV, fashion, movies, adverts, trashy novels and magazines. Eustacia is a 'victim', like everyone else, who falls for the easy solutions proposed by a materialist culture. Of course, TV, fashion, magazines, adverts and movies turn out to be chimeras. TV, glamour, fashion and materialist objects are fakes, masks, paper-thin objects that satisfy no one after they've been consumed.

Eustacia Vye has been seduced by this external, socially-contrived culture, which puts marriage at the top of the ontological pile, the icing on the wedding cake (and wedding cake tastes foul). Eustacia, like Sue Bridehead, has the ability to transcend all this – this culture of towns, labour and marriage, this culture of norms, laws, dogmas and men, the culture that celebrates the middle class, middle-of-the-road living of two-point-four kids in a two-up-two-down on some plastic housing estate in Milton Keynes or Minneapolis with a medium-sized car, living medium-sized lives – everything average, ordinary, normal, deathly. This is death to an artist, a poet, death to anybody like Eustacia Vye. Eustacia is a would-be poet, someone who can transform (her) life. She is a witch, no less, an outsider with hidden powers which she does not know how to activate.

Men can't provide the answers. Nor can society. Transformations, as Ursula Brangwen discovers in *The Rainbow*, have to come from within. No one comes to help you, as Jude Fawley realizes early on in his life (J, I. iv). Eustacia, after yearning for so many years, should know this by now. Perhaps she's just getting round to learning. She is slow – a few more years would do the trick. She must learn to live with frustration and disillusionment. Her story is the story of all people 'growing up' and coming to learn about frustration, and the fact that 'society' has no place for them, does not provide anything that can satisfy their deepest needs. So, in Thoms Hardy's world, everything fails, everything dissatisfies: religion, paganism, labour, education, love, the family, marriage, ambition, friendship and art. There is nothing to rely on. It is all illusion.

VI

Women as 'Mere Chattels': Marty and Grace in *The Woodlanders*

Thomas Hardy enjoyed evoking a closely-knit community, where lives are interlinked, and this is seen very clearly in *The Woodlanders*, where there is a societal hierarchy, from Marty South upwards through Giles Winterbourne, to Grace Melbury, Mr Melbury, Fitzpiers and Felice Charmond. The whole web of characters is connected by economic and material connections (for example, Giles's house, which Mrs Charmond owns). As with *The Mayor of Casterbridge*, there is a deep sense of materialism and economy in *The Woodlanders*. The experiences of labour and production are foregrounded, though given a gloss of romanticism at times, as when Giles and Marty plant seeds, or when Giles stands with his tree at Sherton Abbas market. The economic, social, material and political web of connections are made at times into real objects: there are the totemic or talismanic objects such as Marty's hair, which joins the two ends of the social hierarchy, the top (Charmond) and the bottom (Marty) together; there is Jack South's tree; there is Giles's apple branch; there is the

101

body of Grace's grandmother which Grace 'buys' back from Fitzpiers.

The opening scene, where the barber looks in and sees Marty South in her house, crystallizes a number of themes which preoccupy Hardy: the significance of labour and economy and class; the pleasures of looking, and the secret form of looking, where the observed is unaware of the observer; the relation of narration to visualization; the relations of people from different classes.

Significantly, nearly all the major characters are seen first through the eyes or ears of another character (except for Giles). *The Woodlanders* is a novel of continually shifting viewpoints and mediations. The barber looking at Marty working directly recalls those moments from fairy tales where the heroine is seen living in poverty, doing menial tasks. In Grimms' *Spindle, Shuttle, and Needle* the prince sees his future wife thus:

> *When he came to the house of the poor one, the girl was not at the door but sat inside her little room. He drew rein and looked in at the window, through which the bright sun shone, and saw the girl sitting at her spindle, busily spinning. She looked up, and when she saw the prince looking in, she blushed from head to toe, lowered her eyes, and went on spinning...*[1]

Marty South's hair is, like Tess's mouth, one of the key expressions of her sexuality, so that when Marty cuts off her hair it's seen as a 'rape' that 'deflowers' her ('the rape of her locks'). It is also an act which renders Marty androgynous, and the power of her sexual identity is dramatically reduced by the act, so that she is seen as sexless. Marty is socially, economically and textually marginalized. Her fate – losing her hair, then her dying father, and being left alone at the end of the novel – is the fate of 'a land, a class, and a gender'.[2]

Women are exchanged or bartered in *The Woodlanders*: Grammer Oliver's brain is bought by Fitzpiers; the barber see Marty's hair as worth exploiting; Melbury, the merchant, hopes to make a good trade with his expensively-educated daughter. Each of the women in *The Woodlanders* is evaluated by the men in erotic, social and economic terms. Indeed, it doesn't require an expert in Marxism and materialism to see how brutally (and ambivalently) eroticism is connected to economics.

Marty South is poignantly yearning, and at the end of the novel she is apostrophized by her humble but pure love for Giles. Again, as with Tess, Marty is silenced, and cannot say what she really wants to say: that she loves Giles. While the other characters gush and prattle, Marty keeps quiet. Marty's appearance at the end of *The Woodlanders* is unusual, if one considers how she has been marginalized throughout the narrative. For a long time Marty has been a 'silent absent solitary figure'.[3] The role of the patiently waiting and ever-hopeful lover is usually assigned to men (Diggory Venn, Gabriel Oak, Springrove). Marty trades in her feminine power to assume 'a mystical, classless and sexless identity tested by unfulfilled love and unrecognised labour' (ib., 201). Marty is not frivolous, just as Tess is not frivolous. The treatment of Marty is more severe than Tess, for Marty works for no reward, from any character, while Tess at least enjoys two ecstasies – at Talbothays, and in the 'honeymoon', before she dies.

Money and economics are deeply affected by love in Thomas Hardy's fictive emotional world. Everything is thrown into turmoil by love. When love goes wrong, it injures not only emotions, but everything. It disrupts the flow of life, it injures worldly fortunes, social identity and peer respect. For example, at one point in *The Woodlanders*, Hardy's narrator says that the complications of love affect everyone in Hintock. That is, as in a TV soap opera, everyone is influenced. 'Life among the people involved in the events seemed to be suppressed and hide-bound for a while' (XL). And, another opening sentence to a chapter (XXXIII): '[t]here was agitation that day in the trees of all those whom these matters concerned' (XXXIII).

Women are centrally placed in this socio-economic network of desire. In Thomas Hardy's world, women tease men, make demands of them, chivvy them along; so that, from the men's point of view, they are targets to be nailed down, and 'put in their place'. Hardy's women are disruptive forces, who overturn the moral order of the brotherhoods of labour, government and power. When women enter the male/ masculinist world, they bring unwelcome but yearned-for desires. Hardy's men act and think at times like those members of all-male structures, such as ships, governments, the military, football teams, and so on. One has seen the moment when a woman enters an all-male zone (when she steps on board a ship, a police office, an army barracks) a million times in films. The men look up and scowl. In Mr Melbury's world, Grace's return is seen as disruptive by both the narrator's and the worker's point-of-view. Until Grace arrives, Fitzpiers too is living undisturbed. It's Grace's arrival that begins his fascination for her, to use the word from *The Return of the Native* describing Eustacia's developing interest in Clym Yeobright.

If critics place *The Woodlanders* lower down the hierarchy of Thomas Hardy's novels than some of the others, it is perhaps something to do, again, with intensity. For Grace Melbury's portrayed as a relatively bland person, nowhere near as grand or desirous as Eustacia Vye or Tess Durbeyfield. Indeed, the narrator says it is impossible to describe Grace (V). She seems to be a banal person, until, towards the end, she is fired up with her love for Giles (which she realizes, as all Hardy's characters do, too late). Grace is often treated as lacking in authority and the power to act, even though she does benefit from the social system of privileges. The narrator remarks more than once that Fitzpiers' effect on Grace is an erotic idealization; he is hardly a flesh-and-blood man, but someone '[c]leverer, greater than herself... he seemed to be her ruler rather than her equal, protector, and dear familiar friend' (XIV).

Looking at Grace Melbury more closely, there is more to her than the narrator lets on. The narrator often dismisses her personality and potential, often doing her down in a number of subtle ways. Grace appears stronger when one looks at her in more detail. Grace appears to be sited somewhere between Marty South's 'sexlessness' and the sexiness of Suke Damson and Felice Charmond. Grace is more sexually assertive than critics acknowledge: she enjoys Giles's kisses, and happily joins Fitzpiers in the Sherton Abbas hotel.

Thomas Hardy made a number of changes to *The Woodlanders* in the first collected edition of his works (the Osgood, Mcilvaine edition of 1895). Hardy originally made the novel more sexually explicit: Felice, Suke and Grace were not Fitzpiers' lovers or wives; Grace embraces Giles more passionately, when they think they are clear of Fitzpiers' marriage; Grace is more obvious in her encouragement to Giles that he ought to share his hut with her during the woodland scene; Grace uses more sexually aware terms, such as 'he's had you!' when she's lost in the woods with Mrs Charmond.

Grace Melbury is stuck in such a horrible situation, with *so much* parental pressure on her: the pressure to succeed, to be Mr Melbury's pride and joy. Many times Melbury says he's invested a lot of money in her and expects so much from her in return. She has to lead a double life, being one thing to Giles Winterbourne, another to Melbury, both the village 'maid' and the sophisticated town woman (R. Sumner, 1981, 93). Grace is framed by the patriarchal characters (principally Melbury and Fitzpiers, and Giles) in terms of materialism and sexuality. For Melbury, Grace is not only an 'emotional investment', in the Freudian sense; she is also a financial investment. Melbury expects real, palpable returns from his financial outlay on Grace. This puts her in a difficult position. Hardy makes the œdipal tensions in the father-daughter relation explicitly economic.

Indeed, the œdipal discourse in the book is as powerful as the discourse of heterosexual love. Grace Melbury is under as much emotional pressure from her father as from her two lovers. 'Acquiescence in her father's wishes had been degradation to herself' (XXIX). The parental pressure Mr Melbury exerts is huge, mentioned in nearly every scene in which Melbury appears. It's the same with Mrs Yeobright. These parents are not complete people without the emotions they have for their children. Their children are necessary to make them feel fulfilled. Hence the eternal parental dissatisfaction. For Mrs Yeobright and Mr Melbury, children are a continual disappointment, always falling short of the mark.

In Thomas Hardy's world, one *must* wed, one simply *must wed*, so Melbury never stops forcing Grace to wed. From a character who appears to be 'bland', Grace becomes someone who is pushed about, between each of the three men in her life, Fitzpiers, Giles and Melbury. Each man makes sexual and economic claims on her. It is impossible for her, as for Bathsheba in *Far From the Madding Crowd*, to please all the men in her life. Similarly, Tess is made to feel she has failed her father and her two suitors.

Education does not enhance Grace's life – as far as she can see. '"I have never got any happiness outside Hintock that I know of"' Grace tells her father, and says that '"cultivation has only brought me inconvenience and troubles." (XXX) Oedipal tensions run high not only in the Grace-Melbury relationship, but also in the Jack South and Marty relationship. The cutting down of the tree which obsesses Jack South, for example, links together œdipal conflict, castration, patricide, and the destruction of labour and livelihoods, as well as the forest.

The time scale of *The Woodlanders* revolves around Grace Melbury's sexual liaisons. The seasons are used to highlight and counterpoint the sexual relationships. For instance, Spring is aligned in the traditional manner to courtship as Fitzpiers pursues Grace in the Spring and early Summer. The following Spring, though, Grace has split with Fitzpiers. As with *Tess of the d'Urbervilles*, Hardy constructs a time frame which ironically comments upon the action and themes.

Many times in *The Woodlanders* Grace Melbury speaks in a forthright manner; she is not the 'passive' woman as the narrator depicts her towards the beginning of the novel. For example, Grace tells Fitzpiers that she has had sex with Giles (though it's not true, unlike Fitzpiers' adulteries); she tells her father her education has been unhappy, even a waste of her life; she says she hates being thought of as 'mere chattel', traded between father and prospective husband; Grace is the one who voices the sexual desire that is the foundation of the novel ('"he's had you!"'); she tells her husband that she worships her lover Giles in his death: '"I don't see why you should mind my having had one lover besides yourself in my life, when you have had so many"' (XLVI). The difference being that Fitzpiers slept with his lovers, but Grace did not. Tess is not as blunt as this with Alec, even though critics see her as a much 'stronger' personality than Grace Melbury. Grace's outspokenness on sexual matters at times rivals the most outspoken female voice in all Hardy's fiction, that of Sue Bridehead.

VII

The Rape of Tess:
Sexual Politics in
Tess of the D'Urbervilles

Tess of the d'Urbervilles is a novel of anger, a text which rages against time, God, industrialization, and social institutions such as marriage, Christianity, the Church, law and education. What does Tess do that is 'wrong'? Tom Hardy explains in the book: '[s]he had been made to break an accepted social law, but no law known to the environment in which she fancied herself such an anomaly' (XIII). Tess is forced, or is led, or falls into a complex situation by circumstances, confusions, innocence (or ignorance), bad communication and desire. She is 'made' to break 'an accepted social law': it is the same with Eustacia Vye, or Sue Bridehead. Somehow, their very existence means transgressions will occur. Tess transgresses society, goes against the grain. She (unwittingly perhaps) places herself outside of society and the law. She learns that there are different kinds of laws – different sets of laws for different groups of people. She has to learn about social boundaries, and how to keep inside of limits. The 'law', or 'legal system', does not protect Tess from people like Alec, or from being raped. The law does not right the wrong that has been done to Tess, nor does it punish Alec. As it's a dramatic novel, Tess learns the hard way. She is seen to be transgressive. The education system fails her utterly, and her mother and family also fail to protect her. Though she is proud of her education, it fails her utterly. A note in the *Life* is usually cited in relation to *Tess of the d'Urbervilles*: '[w]hen a married woman who has a lover kills her husband, she does not really wish to kill her husband; she wishes to kill the situation' (289). I concentrate in this chapter on Tess's rape, the first Phases of the book, and her relations with Alec and Angel.

Feminist critics have noted how the narrator of *Tess of the d'Urbervilles* is himself deeply (sometimes jealously and ambiguously) in love with his heroine. The intensity of the reader's identification with Tess Durbeyfield can be seen in much of Hardy criticism. J. Hillis Miller, a respected Hardy critic, writes in *Fiction and Repetition*: 'I for one find the description of Angel Clare's failure to consummate his marriage to Tess almost unbearably painful' (1982, 119).

A couple of inter-connected points are worth making about this revealing comment; firstly, it is that of a male critic, who is relating to a deeply sexualized female character – the intensity of the critic's identification may be related to the assumed gender of the critic and the character; secondly, the male critic assumes the significance of sexual consummation to be enormous. Sex must be crucial to the critic, because he finds it 'unbearably painful' when Tess doesn't get the sexual consummation the critic thinks she desires.

One critic suggested that Thomas Hardy was so protective of Tess he deliberately had her keep her distance, sexually, from Angel and Alec. For another critic, Hardy's identification with Tess, when it's so intense, can exonerate her of her mistakes (L. Claridge, 324f). *Tess of the d'Urbervilles*'s narrator may start out describing events from the detached position of a topographer or historian, but soon his disinterestedness is overtaken by an erotic gaze as he looks at Tess, isolates her from other clubwalkers, and describes her eyes and 'mobile peony mouth' (later on,

108

Tess's eyes are described as having 'ever-varying pupils, with their radiating fibrils of blue, and black, and gray, and violet' XXVII). Alec's erotic gaze is the one that marks Tess, not Angel's, and this image of Tess – as eroticized and colonized by a vulgar, shallow male – becomes the basis of her image in the rest of the book. It is as if Alec imprinted his gaze on Tess first, not Angel (K. Silverman, 1984). Angel did see her first – but not fully, only as a maiden standing slightly apart from the other dancers at Marlott. The narrator notes that it was sad that Angel did not connect with Tess first.

Part of the pressure of the narrator upon Tess is phallic, with its tropes of penetration and piercing (the rosethorn, Prince's death, and so on). The narrator describes ways in to Tess's body – through her eyes, mouth and skin. For Penny Boumelha, the 'narrator's erotic fantasies of penetration and engulfment enact a pursuit, violation and persecution of Tess in parallel with those she suffers at the hands of her two lovers' (1982, 120). The authorial pressure upon Tess, and especially upon her body, make her 'not just discursively determined, but discursively *overdetermined*' (K. Silverman, i1984). Hardy's texts are 'overdetermined', Hillis Miller noted, due to their 'too many irreconcilable' elements (1982, 128).

For feminist critics, the important parts of the book Thomas Hardy changed were Tess's character. Tess was originally called Sue, Love, Cis and also Rose Mary. She was called Love Woodrow, Cis Woodrow and sometimes Sue Troublewell. She was later Rose-Mary Troublefield. The name d'Urberville was originally 'Hawnferne' (it become 'Turberville' before it became 'd'Urberville'). Early titles for the novel were *Too Late Beloved,* and *Too Late, Beloved!*. The resonance of the phrase 'too late beloved' occurs in the Sandbourne scene when Angel returns. Tess spoke standard English rather than the dialect, which was added later (H, 19). She became more and more significant for Hardy, it seems, as her 'innocence' and 'chastity' were emphasized. She was 'purified' – 'Tess's purity... is "stuck on"' says Mary Jacobus (1978, 78). Hardy apparently made the differences between Alec and Tess more extreme – they were more like 'equals' in earlier versions of the story.

In one view, Tess Durbeyfield herself brings together most of Thomas Hardy's women characters: the submissive type, the 'flirt', the *femme fatale*, the 'victim', the idealistic lover, and the would-be teacher or educated woman (P. Boumelha, 1982, 117). Tess is exalted, at various times, as a poet, as a martyr, as a saint (during the baptism), as a religious rebel (again, at the baptism, and afterwards with Angel), as an archetypal 'fallen woman', as a sensuous nature lover, as a fecund Goddess. There is Tess the would-be school teacher; Tess the 'milkmaid'; Tess the worker; Tess the 'wronged maiden' of balladry; Tess the 'good-girl, governness-type heroine of Victorian convention' (E. Moers, 1967); there is Tess the unconventional single mother; Tess the murderer; Tess the 'victim'; Tess the prostitute; Tess the proto-New Woman; Tess the Earth Mother; and Tess the aristocratic d'Urberville, doomed, romantic, noble, yet enduring (Ellen Moers says this stereotype 'may have been Hardy's favourite' [1967]).

Thomas Hardy made everything relatively clear in *Tess of the d'Urbervilles* – he did not make the main parts of the story deliberately mysterious. For example, Hardy's use of symbolism is pretty basic. For instance, Alec says '"my arms [are] a lion rampant"' (V). Instead of saying the d'Urberville heraldic arms are a rampant lion Hardy might as well have said a rampant phallus, 'all the better to eat you with', as the wolf says to Little Red Riding Hood.

From the very first description of Tess, she is eroticized by the narrator. As the all-seeing, voyeuristic eye of the narrator roves over the sisterhood of club-walkers, it closes in and rests on Tess, drawing attention to her 'mobile peony mouth' (II). The eroticization of Tess's mouth and body occurs partly because Thomas Hardy cannot depict sex acts, so his narrator displaces attention to Tess's body, descriptions which can get past the censor. In doing so, Tess's erotic body is simultaneously exalted and suppressed, spoken and silenced. As Mary Jacobus puts it, '[t]hough Hardy seems to be salvaging Tess's body for spirituality (the vessel is brim-full), the yawning mouth opens up a split in the very terms he uses' (1986, 31).

Like many male narrators, *Tess of the d'Urbervilles'* narrator is fascinated by what is inside Tess's body, the great unknown of Freudian psychoanalysis – that is, female sexuality. The problem is that, as French feminists such as Luce Irigaray and Hélène Cixous noted, female sexuality is unrepresentable in patriarchal culture. Thus, the closer Hardy's narrator gets to Tess's erotic interior, the less can be said about it. Instead, Tess's body becomes part of the male narcissistic process, that is, a mirror in which men see their narcissism reflected. (Not only Angel and Alec see their narcissism reflected in Tess, but also Tess's father, with his dream of her continuing the d'Urberville heritage, and other male characters). As Margaret Higonnet asks of *Tess*, '[c]an a man implicated in patriarchy speak for a woman constrained by it?'[1]

Tess of the d'Urbervilles takes the breaking of a social law and develops it as a number of ricochets. The initial rape develops into narratives concerning having sex before marriage, having a child outside wedlock, trying to live outside of society and Christianity, lying to one's betrothed, living in sin, and finally murder. Religion is not automatically dominant in the rural community, though: as one critic put it, 'although almost all the characters attend church [in *Tess*], they do not believe in or understand Christian dogma' (N. Schoenburg, 1989).

The text opposes culture with nature: the narrator seems to be on the side of nature. Culture, embodied in Angel's ardent religiosity and Alec's fake knowledge, is dangerous. It upsets the time-honoured equilibrium of the rural world. Nature is prized above culture, perhaps, because it seems to be more in tune with life. Though it is the men who are often the culture bearers, it is the women who actually yearn more, are more socially ambitious. What men offer in Hardy's texts is a cultural sophistication which, finally, the women, nor the men, do not want. Tess, at one of her lowpoints, repeats to herself that '[a]ll is vanity'. However, she goes on consider that '[a]ll was, alas, worse than vanity – injustice, punishment, exaction, death' (XLI). Nature is not free from pain and complications in Hardy's fictive world: in fact, everything hurts. Love, marriage, work, religion, nature – all have pain. In the *Life* Hardy wrote: '[p]ain has been, and pain is' (315). The women in the Talbothays bedroom writhe 'feverishly under the oppressiveness of an emotion thrust on them by cruel Nature's law' (XXIII). But pain = being alive in the Western (masculinist) tradition, and the most exquisite sort of pain in Hardy's fictive world is being in love. Love = pain = life. The point about Tess is that she is fully alive: 'she *lives* what paper-poets write' (XXVI). Tess is seen as being more fully alive than the male characters in the narrative. The exaltation of women in the novel, though, is double-edged. Tess embodies much that men exalt in women, and she suffers because of it. Tess, for example, deliberately makes herself ugly, to escape the lecherous looks of men (XLII). Ironically, when Tess is deprived of Angel's gaze, she slips into melancholy. Angel's allegorizing (and erotic) gaze is important in stabilizing Tess's self-image.[2] Tess lives fully in her body, but Alec indulges his negligently, and Angel is scarcely aware of his (he brushes aside the discomforts of his Brazilian adventure). What Angel demands and Tess cannot deliver is the pure, idealized body. Tess's body goes through much: rape, pregnancy, childbirth, her child's death, labouring and travelling.

Tess is a problematic novel, gender-wise, because 'Hardy appears to lay much of the blame for [Tess's] difficulties on the body' (L. Pykett). Julia Kristeva's reading of the Christian crucifixion is pertinent to the sense of bodily suffering in Hardy's heroines (in particular Tess Durbeyfield)). For Kristeva, the moment of agony in the Crucifixion and its immediate aftermath is usefully regarded in terms of a psychoanalytic feminism:

> *Since resurrection there is, and, as Mother of God, she must know this, nothing justifies Mary's outburst of pain at the foot of the cross, unless it be the desire to experience within her own body the death of a human being, which her feminine fate of being the source of life spares her. Could it be that love, as puzzling as it is ancient, of mourners for corpses relates to the same longing of a woman whom nothing fulfills – the longing to experience the wholly masculine pain of a man who expires at every moment on account of jouissance due to obsession with his own death? And yet, Marian pain is in no way connected with tragic outburst: joy and even a kind of triumph follow upon tears, as if the conviction that death does not exist were an irrational but unshakable maternal certainty, on which the principle of resurrection had to rest. (Tales of Love, 250-1)*

Tess's suffering can be seen as out of proportion with her mistakes or 'crimes'. After the rape and sorrowful motherhood, 'as Hardy sees it, there is no reason in nature for Tess to receive further punishment' (B. Sankey, 1965; A. LaValley, 95). Yet she does. The 'causes' of Tess's tragedy, seen within the narrative, in terms of events, often seem trivial or at last relatively minor. For example, one of the 'causes' for Tess to climb up with Alec on his horse before the rape is her argument with Car Darch. Tess's d'Urberville pride asserts itself here, as she tries to raise herself above the workers. But Tess's mistake at this point, to try to keep aloof, is not commensurate with her subsequent 'punishment', her rape.

In *Tess of the d'Urbervilles*, 'sham' marriages (Alec and Tess) are followed by legal but sexually/ spiritually damaged marriages (Angel and Tess), then another legal marriage (a trick marriage, not desired by Tess), then the spiritual and sexual consummation in the empty house. One 'marriage' ironically and ambivalently modulates the one before. The narrative reads something like this: '(Unconsummated) marriage > (adulterous) "marriage" > (Alec's) death > (consummated) marriage > (Tess's) death > (Angel's implied re-)marriage' (D. Sadoff, 156).

Scapegoats are required, though. '"Once victim, always victim – that's the law"' (XLVII). The point is that *all* the people in *Tess of the d'Urbervilles* are victims. It is just not Tess Durbeyfield who is trapped into a certain way of thinking and acting, but also Alec, Angel, Mrs Durbeyfield, Farmer Groby, and so on. There is spontaneity, freedom, 'nature', but such openness is continually crushed by socialized ways of thinking and doing. Tess retains her openness and potential, even at the end, which is why she is a 'pure woman'. She still believes in happiness at the end of the novel, astonishingly. She is indomitable. She speaks of the 'sweet and lovely' time she and Angel have in the empty house (LVIII). She knows, too, as she wakes up on the sacrifical stone at Stonehenge, that '[t]his happiness could not have lasted' (LVIII). Though a 'victim', Tess experiences rapture, is loved and loathed, is perhaps the most alive of Thomas Hardy's characters.

Tess Durbeyfield is a scandalous figure, as far as Victorian society was concerned.[3] She is offensive to Victorian sensibility – she is raped, she lives in sin and adultery, she is openly sexual, a religious sceptic and finally, a murderer (K. Blake, 1982, 690). Yet she is 'pure': Thomas Hardy bids the reader remember 'the meaning of the word in Nature' and the æsthetic and Christian uses of the term 'pure' (T, 38). By 'pure', Hardy means honest – she is true to herself. It is when the word 'pure' is associated with openly sexual and transgressive behaviour that the problems begin with such a definition.

Tess of the d'Urbervilles is a proto-feminist text in its challenging of societal norms. It rewrites the 'wronged maiden' ballad narrative,[4] the fairy tale quality of the text, where the princess must marry her prince at the end. Thomas Hardy's *Tess* recalls *Little Red Riding Hood, Bluebeard* and *Sleeping Beauty*. Other similarities between *Tess of the d'Urbervilles* and *Little Red Riding Hood*: in a country setting a mother sends her young, virginal daughter on an errand to an old woman; both Tess and Little Red Riding Hood are marked by the colour red (Tess is linked with a red ribbon, strawberries, roses, blood, and so on); like the wolf, Alec diverts Tess's attention with masses of flowers; Alec acts like the wolf, with his predatory manner, his 'bold rolling eye' and sly, patronizing language ('Well, my Beauty', 'my pretty Coz'); as in *Little Riding Hood*, the food Tess eats 'in a half-pleased, half-reluctant state' (V) hints at sexual acts.

Other affinities between Thomas Hardy's fiction and fairy tales include: poverty; the rural settings; the useless father (in *Hansel and Gretel*); the dark forest; the Stoke-d'Urberville mansion as a (fake) fairy tale castle; older women envying young female beauty (in *The Woodlanders* and *Snow White*); family curses; potential violence; and the dream of perfect romance.

As in *Little Red Riding Hood*, a forest features prominently in *Tess of the d'Urbervilles*: the 'tragic' event in Tess's relations with Alec, the rape, occurs in a forest. And not just any forest, but one of England's ancient woodlands, significantly known as The Chase. Tess is seen by the narrator as a prey to the hunter, as virgin or conquerable territory to the soldier, as a victim to the sadist, and as a sacrifical lamb to society (D. Sadoff, 156). The theme of hunting is evoked a number of times by the narrator,[5] not least in portraying Alec as a mock-squire predator. Even before the Trantridge episodes, Hardy's narrator in chapter two describes this part of Dorset as the Vale of the White Hart. The casually related anecdote of a mediæval legend, about a hunter killing 'a beautiful white hart' that was spared by Henry III and being fined for it, is of course not at all casual, but bears directly on Tess's fate. The identification between the hunted hart and hunted woman (the soft, white female object penetrated by the phallic axe or spear) also chimes with *Snow White and the Seven*

114

Dwarfs.

In *Tess of the d'Urbervilles,* many of the faults and mistakes come from men, from masculine discourses, and from patriarchal institutions, such as marriage and the Church. Tess (naively it turns out) expects to find a decently behaved human being who will return her love. What she gets is one man who rapes her and dominates her socially and psychologically, and another man who cannot accept all of her, her past, her body and sexuality, her desires. Tess asks too much of her suitors: she wishes for too much as a fairy tale princess: she wishes for love. She gives love, time after time, but receives a jaundiced, selfish, fetishized sort of love in return.

In *The Newly Born Woman,* what Hélène Cixous writes about intention and desire applies directly to Tess's fate: '[i]ntention: desire, authority – examine them and you are led right back...to the father.' So that '[e]ither woman is passive or she does not exist. What is left of her is unthinkable, unthought' (1994, 39). Cytherea Graye is also 'passive', remaining throughout much of *Desperate Remedies* in a constrained position. When Tess returns to her mother and cries '"[w]hy didn't you tell me there was danger in men-folk?"' (XII), it is a terribly direct question. It is the sort of question one finds in Arthurian romance (such as 'what do women want?' – 'sovereignty' was Georges Bataille's suggestion). Tess's question goes to the heart of Hardy's theme (the inhumanity of humanity), and to the heart of feminism. Intolerance is his great theme, as it is with feminists such as Andrea Dworkin, Mary Daly, Susan Griffin and Luce Irigaray.

The writing of Tess's rape reveals some key changes which Hardy made in later drafts:

> *Darkness & silence ruled everywhere around. Above them rose*
> > in which were poised
> *the primeval yews & oaks of the Chase, & the gentle roosting*
> > all about
> *birds in their last nap; & around them were the hopping rabbits & hares.*
> *But where was*
> > Rose Mary's Tess's
> *Sue's guardian angel; where was Providence? Perhaps, like that*
> *other god of*

ironical

whom the Tishbite spoke, he was talking, or he was pursuing... (from folio 99; J. Laird, 73)

The early scenes of *Tess of the d'Urbervilles* are exquisite, but so apparently 'simple', it's a wonder that Hardy dared to write them. That is, the depictions – of Tess Durbeyfield and her sisterhood dancing in the field, John and Joan Durbeyfield in Rolliver's Inn, Tess and Abraham on the cart, and so on – seem close to being so simple they're quaint and sentimental. All the time, though, Hardy's narrator invests the scenes with ironies and hints at future complications and sadness. It is Tess's personality, primarily, that embodies the reservations in the narrative. She is not convinced about her mother's enthusiasm for the relations at Trantridge, and is not impressed by her father's easy acceptance of being a noble d'Urberville. It is her father's revelling in the news, for example, that has him celebrating at Rolliver's and not being in a fit state to take the beehives to Casterbridge. Tess resents this debauchery. '"O my God! Go to a public-house to get up his strength!"' (III) It would be easy, in another context, to see Tess as the tiresome family conscience, someone a little stuck-up, who must be humoured but ignored (in fact, her mother does partly ignore Tess's highmindedness).

It is also Jack Durbeyfield's clinging onto being 'Sir John' while doing nothing about it that encourages Tess to go to Trantridge. 'His reasons for staying away were worse to Tess than her own objection to going' (V). There are a number of reasons mooted why Tess does go to 'claim kin' – but the major reason is not that her mother wishes to have her find a husband; neither is it the ignoble task, as Durbeyfield sees it, of asking for help from well-off relatives; no, it is that Tess killed the horse and has to make good the crime. The narrator notes this burning coal in Tess's conscience a number of times. For example, when Alec charges over the hill in the gig, to pick up Tess, she hesitates. The narrator suggests that one of the things that decides her to step into Alec's dog cart, instead of taking the slow cart, is the sight of her family watching from a distance and 'possibly the thought that she had killed Prince' (VII).

These early scenes are very poignant, especially Tess's leavetaking, which is seen from the viewpoint of the mother and her children. With an economy of words, the narrator suggests that Tess is moving out of her depth, and far out of the little enclosed world of Marlott and the Vale of Blackmore. The departure of Tess from her family takes place on a hill, at the boundary of the two regions, the Vale of Blackmore and the Trantridge region.

The horseplay at the beginning of *Tess of the d'Urbervilles* expresses age-old heterosexual oppositions: Tess has a male horse called Prince; Alec has a mare called Tib (a palindrome of 'bit'). The configuration of horses to humans doesn't need commentary – it underlines the sexual politics of the novel. For example, Tess's horse is a tired old workhorse, essential for the family's survival; Alec's horse is primarily for his leisure. Alec's mare is significant, too, in chapter I. viii, in presaging the horse ride into The Chase and Tess's rape.

What happens is Alec intercepts Tess on her journey to Trantridge and persuades her to ride with him. At this point, the sexual metaphor of 'riding' hardly needs pointing out. The erotic undercurrent is made clear when Alec is all for racing down the hills, while Tess holds back. Tib the mare becomes an equivalent for Tess's dubious situation, for Alec says she is a wild horse that must be mastered, and he has the power to do it (VIII). Further, Alec's mare has killed a man, and nearly killed Alec: the situation echoes Tess's own destiny in the novel.

The horse ride to Trantridge, when the sexual relations between Tess and Alec begin (with the 'kiss of mastery'), looks forward to the rape scene: Tess's white muslin dress is blown 'to her very skin', and in the violation scene, Tess is seen as a 'white muslin figure' (XI). During the ride on the gig, the banks of the straight road look like a splitting stick (I. viii). The metaphor is vivid: it looks forward to the moment when Alec will penetrate Tess, splitting her body apart. The arguments on the Trantridge horse ride – whether or not to put her arm around him for safety, whether or not to ride with him – foreshadow the rape and her relations with Alec. Alec calls her a 'young witch', an 'artful hussy', and 'called her everything he could think of' (VIII). Alec will always call Tess a whore, it is one of his many acts of violence against her.

Much of the argument in this scene stems from Alec's request for a kiss

– in Victorian literature, as in much other art, a kiss is a synecdoche, standing in for sex. Tess's reply is straightforward: '"[b]ut I don't want anybody to kiss me, sir!"' (VIII) and she begins to cry. Poor Tess: saying no is not enough, and Alec gives her 'the kiss of mastery' anyway (VIII). As with the rape, Tess tries to wipe off the mark of his kiss, just as Car Darch tries to wipe the imprint of the sticky treacle off her back. Of the 'kiss of mastery', the narrator says that Tess tries to rub it away: '[s]he had, in fact, undone the kiss, as far as such a thing was physically possible' (VIII).

The kiss, of course, cannot be 'undone', even less can the rape be 'undone'. Tess finds that being raped is an immense psychological scar that cannot be wiped away; and neither can being pregnant be 'undone'. For Tess, a huge social gulf opens between the person she was before Trantridge and the changed woman she is afterwards. Tess vows to return to her mother as she argues with Alec about riding with him. This is the point at which she could return, after being called a whore; but then her social conscience reminds her that she could not go back on such 'sentimental grounds' (VIII).

Tess's rape destroys the wholeness of the female body. It is an inscription which she can never erase. She tries, with her confession, to revenge her violation, but it doesn't work. The bitter irony of *Tess of the d'Urbervilles* is that even the murder of Alec does not erase the rape. How can it? The damage has already been done.

During Tess's short time at The Slopes, Alec continues to insult her and stalk her. He follows her around, spies on her, even hiding behind a curtain at one point. Alec says that she offers him 'such temptation as never before fell to mortal man' (IX), making the first of many allusions in the novel to Adam, Eve and the Fall. Indeed, the narrator of *Tess* reminds the reader that, between 'Phase the First' and 'Phase the Second', after the rape, Tess 'learnt that the serpent hisses where the sweet birds sing, and her views of life had been totally changed for her by the lesson' (XII). The masses of caged birds at Trantridge need no gloss as another equivalence of Tess's state – later on comparisons are made between Tess and caged animals, or animals on the run (as when she kills the pheasants out of mercy).

It is ironic that one of the forces that persuades Tess Durbeyfield to climb onto Alec's horse again should be female sexual jealousy and resentment. Just as Tess's mother encouraged her to further her career via her sexual charms (her face or 'beauty'), so 'dark Car', the Queen of Spades, resents Tess's reserve which she sees as haughtiness. Again, Tess gets called a 'hussy', this time by Car Darch, who perceives Tess as a sexual rival. Tess does not see herself in this light at all, but in the unreality of the strange moonlit night, such subtleties are lost.

Car Darch's method of getting the treacle stain off her back is of course a grotesque parody of the sexual act ('spinning horizontally on the herbage and dragging herself over it upon the elbows', X). Car Darch's wriggling again presages Tess's fate during the rape an hour or two later. When Alec arrives on the fight scene class relations are suddenly reinforced, the revellers sober up and collect themselves to continue homeward. Tess's predicament is immense: '[a]t any other moment of her life she would have refused such proffered aid and company' (X). The act of accepting a ride with Alec a second time is seen as another of Tess's mistakes.

In the run-up to the rape, in the next chapter (I. XI), the narrator is firmly on Tess's side. He describes how Tess has been up at five each day that week, has been on her feet all day, has waited for three hours without food or drink (XI). She is exhausted, at one of her many low points in the narrative. The narrator does allow Alec a certain integrity, in having Alec saying he feels 'responsible for [Tess's] safe conduct home' (XI). But this effort at nobility of Alec's comes after he has let the horse wander miles away, instead of taking Tess straight home. Alec's statements just before the rape imply that he did not intend to rape Tess, that he was merely enjoying riding on the horse with her.

But then the narrator turns his attention to Tess as Alec returns: she is 'a pale nebulousness' in her white muslin dress (XI); she is absorbed back into the landscape, as far as the male gaze is concerned (K. Silverman, 1984); she is asleep and has been weeping, as if she has already guessed at Alec's real intention in bringing her to such an isolated spot (XI). Then the narrator stresses Tess's virginity, using the classic metaphor of untrammelled white snow upon which is 'traced such a coarse pattern'

119

(XI). Hardy's narrator depicts the scene as a man taking Tess's virginity against her will: in many feminists' views, this is defined as rape. The fact that it's rape is indisputable: the power relations between the two have already been emphasized by *Tess*'s narrator: the 'kiss of mastery', the power struggle with the mare Tib, the class superiority of the man, the man forcing fruit and flowers on Tess, and so on. The rape is a continuation of these male-female power relations.

Thomas Hardy's is a literature of loss. In *Tess of the d'Urbervilles*, everything fails: love, motherhood, ambition, folklore, custom, history, tradition, matriarchy. They all fail, or are lost. In Hardy's fiction, the most piquant loss is loss of love. In *Jude the Obscure*, in Jude's first experience of erotic love, a Lacanian lack or void opens up inside him. 'She was not there now' the narrator says, so that 'a void was in his heart which nothing could fill' (I. vii). The irony is, with love comes the void, and the more one desires, the greater the hunger and the void becomes. Tess, as the virgin Angel imagines her to be, i.e., Tess as representation, 'makes good male lack through the fantasmatic restoration of phenomenal plenitude' said Kaja Silverman (1984). Tess's loss is her innocence, her virginity and childhood. '"Why didn't you warn me?"' she asks her mother (XII). Parents are often blamed. But parents are not trained to be parents – they have to learn as much as children do. Except they don't.

Nature's law, in Thomas Hardy's ideology, is that parents have to push children out into the world to learn the hard way, by the thousand natural shocks. Hardy's point, which is his central argument, is that many of the most harmful knocks are not 'natural' at all, but made by humans. Nature's law is: live, and live now. There is no second thought, no delay. Tess learns that most of the hard knocks come from people – even from herself (she was negligent and was partly responsible for the horse Prince's death).

Another way of stating the dilemma in *Tess of the d'Urbervilles* is 'the wrong man the woman, the wrong woman the man' (XI). As the rape is in progress, Thomas Hardy sidetracks with a philosophical discourse. Why is it, the narrator asks, that things go wrong? (XI) Tess Durbeyfield later takes the rape in a fatalistic way, like the rural inhabitants: 'it happened'.

Is it rape in *Tess of the d'Urbervilles*? Obviously it is. Tess is taken into pitch darkness, having not even kissed a man in a sexual manner, and is raped. This is utter horror. Not only is Tess raped, she becomes pregnant from this first sexual encounter. The rape makes manifest the patriarchal power of men, in a brutal way. Tess has to learn – and quickly – that men have certain powers and privileges that must not be questioned. If one does question them, they'll shut you up – either men themselves, or their laws.

This is exactly what happens to Tess. Like so many rape 'victims', she keeps quiet about it, naming neither the act nor the rapist. Tess doesn't blab, except to her mother, the one person she hoped would save her, or at least warn her.[6] For some feminists (often Anglo-American feminists) rape is a crime and a social institution which perpetrates patriarchal power. Marriage is sanctified rape in this view (one see this so clearly in Alec's later repossession of Tess, but also in Angel's view of Tess: he calls her 'this little womanly thing... What I become, she must become. What I cannot be, she cannot be"' XXXIV). Both *Tess of the d'Urbervilles* and *Jude the Obscure* examine in detail the idea of marriage as legitimized rape.

Andrea Dworkin's outraged analysis of rape fits so well at times with the proto-feminist discourse of *Tess of the d'Urbervilles* and *Jude the Obscure*. For example, this passage from *Right-Wing Women*:

> *The propaganda stresses that intercourse can give a woman pleasure if she does it right: specially if she has the right attitude toward it and toward the man. The right attitude is to want it. The right attitude is to desire men* because *they engage in phallic penetration. The right attitude is to want intercourse because men want it. The right attitude is not to be selfish: especially about orgasm.* (1983, 81)

This describes the state of so many female characters in so many classic novels, by George Eliot or Charles Dickens or Jane Austen or Emily Brontë or Virginia Woolf, or Thomas Hardy. Regarding the heroines of 'classic' novels – Clarissa, Tess Durbeyfield, Eustacia Vye, Catherine Earnshaw, Connie Chatterley – Dworkin's aggressive analyses of marriage seems to describe an important part of women's sexual economy:

In marriage a man has the sexual right to his wife: he can fuck her at will by right of law. The law articulates and defends this right. The state articulates and defends this right. This means that the state defines the intimate uses of a woman's body in marriage; so that a man acts with the protection of the state when he fucks his wife, regardless of the degree of force surrounding or intrinsic to the act... But even where marital rape is illegal, the husband has at his disposal the ordinary means of sexual coercion, including threat of physical violence, punitive economic measures, sexual or verbal humiliation in private or in public, violence against inanimate objects, and threats against children. In other words, eliminating the legal sanctioning of rape does not in itself eliminate sexual coercion in marriage; but the continued legal sanctioning of rape underlines the coercive character and purpose of marriage. Marriage law is irrefutable proof that women are not equal to men. (1983, 77-78)

Dworkin's concern, like Thomas Hardy's and other politically and socially committed writers, is oppression, and she has no doubts as to who is the oppressor, and what arguments the oppressor uses to further the cause of oppression:

The oppressor, the one who perpetrates the wrongs for his own pleasure or profit, is the master inventor of justification. He is the magician who, out of thin air, fabricates wondrous, imposing, seemingly irrefutable intellectual reasons which explain why one group must be degraded at the hands of another. (1988, 198)

A typical view of *Tess of the d'Urbervilles* is that the heroine is a sacrifice to appease society (J.J. Lecercle).[7] Tess's function is also a scapegoat, someone who can be kicked now and then to satisfy the violence of others. Most of those others are male. Tess Durbeyfield is the object of many males' fantasies and violence – Alec and Angel mainly, but also the farmer, and the lecherous youth in the Chalk-Newton inn (XLII). Tess's mother, as well as men, sees Tess as a sexual object, an item of exchange with Alec d'Urberville. As Luce Irigaray writes, '[w]omen, signs, goods, currency, all pass from one man to another'.[8] Tess is passed around like a commodity with a high use-value (while she is sexually active – after that, older women are often abandoned). Tess's whole environment is thoroughly patriarchal. There are only a few enclaves of sisterhood, such as the milkmaids at Talbothays. Even then, though, the sisterhood's talk is mainly of Angel Clare and 'compulsory heterosexuality' (Adrienne Rich's term).

Tess's predicament is terrible because, like so many battered wives or abused people, 'she had no counsellor' (XXXIII). She has no one to confide in, as with Bathsheba, Eustacia, Grace Melbury and Elizabeth-Jane. She is alone. Even the potentially powerful Talbothays sisterhood doesn't help her with her main problem. Tess has to learn about the pain of loneliness. 'But nobody did come, because nobody does' as the narrator of *Jude the Obscure* says (I. iv). Tess has to learn self-sufficiency.

Even so, after the rape, she goes back to work for her parents (something Alec and Angel do not do). The life view in *Tess of the d'Urbervilles* is very narrow: the people in the rural regions think of love and labour, gossip and marriage, and little else. Tess seems to be different from others with her perception of the stars, or the eternal sunrises. She cannot, though, escape the immense patriarchal pressures around her: to work, to conform, to marry, to have a family. And the pursuit of marriage becomes work in Hardy's world. These may be social lies – the merits of labour and marriage – but all Hardy's protagonists have to wrestle with them.

Tess, as a scapegoat, is subject to male projection, where men project onto women their faults and weaknesses. Feminists call this 'satanism' or 'demonization'. Whatever goes wrong, it must be the fault of women – hence Conservative politicians in Britain in the 1990s singling out young unmarried mothers as scroungers.[9] How could men, with their high ideals and desensitized personalities, be the 'guilty' ones? Tess takes upon herself the guilt. This is the obscenity of the novel, Hardy's 'offensive truth'.

Angel backs up her guilt when he rejects her after the confession scene. He prefers a literary, mythical Tess; not a flesh and blood woman, but a Goddess, a literary creation. Via her confession, Tess forces Angel to confront her actual body, and to delete his spiritualized image of her: for Angel, Tess's body can 'incite more than one allegorization, thus putting both the validity and the uniqueness of his reading into question'.[10] Tess as Woman as image or text ('tex').

The problem is that men sexualize and fetishize everything – not just women. Both Alec and Angel see Tess in sexual terms, first and foremost.

Their fetishized vision of Tess controls most of their attitudes towards her and their actions. Alec sees Tess as a pleasure ground in which he can satisfy his lust. Later on, Alec calls Tess a whore in numerous ways. Angel views Tess in similarly fetishized, erotic terms. Angel cannot handle her rape: it forces him to confront face-on her sexuality, and his sexualization of her. Rape is affirmed in patriarchal society, according to feminists. Tess's problem is therefore society's problem: she has to speak the unspeakable. She has to say 'I have been raped'. But no one wants to hear it, or can hear it. Worse, Tess cannot say it: she is continually silenced. She has to tell Angel 'you, Angel, and society, condemn me. And you are all wrong'.

As Hélène Cixous writes: '[w]omen should break out of the snare of silence. They should not be conned into accepting a domain which is the margin or the harem' (E. Marks, 251). For Wayne Anderson, silence is central to Hardy's fiction: he claims that the rhetoric of Hardy's fiction is fundamentally 'a rhetoric of silence' (1985, 54). Sometimes Tess is seen grappling with clichés, such as the one that Alec suggests: that women mean yes, sexually, when they say no. Tess's task is partly to reclaim language and the ability to express oneself (A. Poole, 342). Even when Tess does speak, she is ignored. Sometimes her silence indicates guilt and the suppression of her past; at other times it indicates resentment, eroticism or dumb subordination (H, 21).

One critic relates Tess's predicament to the tension between desire and language in Julia Kristeva's philosophy.[11] There are key moments when forthright statements are required, but not made. For example, when Arabella returns from Oz, and asks Jude what they ought to do, Jude drinks and lets Arabella lead him to a bout of sex in Aldbrickham, instead of making for an immediate divorce. One strong word about divorce might save him – because the very next day, Sue marries Phillotson. Similarly, the narrative of *Tess of the d'Urbervilles* is crying out for Tess to tell Angel about her former life, before their relationship becomes too far advanced, but she doesn't.

At the mid-point of the narrative, Tess's confession, there is much to discuss, and the honeymoon scene is packed with dialogue. Angel begins by patronizing Tess, calling her 'this little womanly thing' (XXXIV). Here, though, it is clearly Angel Clare who is the 'little boyish thing'. Tess is still trying to sympathize and empathize with Angel: she considers him her double when he says he too has something to confess (ib.). He proves not to be her double or equal. Tess forgives Angel's premeditated sex with a stranger, while he cannot forgive her being raped. While it's OK for the man to fuck around, in a deliberate, conscious manner, it is not OK for the woman to be raped against her will. Tess turns into the fallen woman here, Eve, the temptress who brings down her ideal mate. Angel excuses his 'eight-and-forty hours dissipation with a stranger', even though, in terms of his Pauline Christianity, it is condemned. Tess's rape, meanwhile, which ought to be pitied and forgiven, or whatever it is Angel Clare does in his religion, is suppressed. Tess has to learn to 'lie or die', as Andrea Dworkin puts it.[12] At this point, where Tess is silenced by Angel, she is also silenced by the novel: there is a break between 'Phase the Fourth', 'The Consequence' and 'Phase the Fifth', 'The Woman Pays'. Just when Tess begins to tell her story, there are blank pages.

The blank pages between each Phase are critical, occurring during her rape, and her confession. Thomas Hardy did not put them there for no reason. The first break, between the first two Phases, is reasonably straightforward: Hardy's narrator has laid the framework for the narrative, and the titles of the two Phases – 'The Maiden' and 'Maiden No More' – seem to explain what has occurred in this first break. What may be in dispute is how much the event was a 'seduction' or a 'rape'. If one goes back over the 'Phase the First', one can put forward arguments for rape or seduction or whatever. For most feminists, though, Tess Durbeyfield is raped, and the break in the text serves to illuminate the event by its very omission. Hardy made it clearer in subsequent editions of *Tess* that force was used in the 'seduction' scene. He added the words which depicted Alec leaning down to Tess's face and finding tears. Afterwards, one of the fieldwomen, in another addition to the original, mentions that '"[a] little more than persuading had to do wi' the coming o't, I reckon"' (XIV; J. Laird, 176). The reader has already seen Alec forcing Tess to accept a strawberry from Alec, a symbolically weighted moment which offers an equivalent for the rape, like Prince's death (see A. Brick, 1962, 118). For some critics, the gaps between the Phases hint at

Hardy pre-censoring the narrative so that adverse opinions of Tess cannot be formed.[13]

For other critics, the gaps indicate how Tess's sexuality evades being described by the narrative voice (J. Bayley, 189; P. Boumelha, 1982, 126-7). One can see how Tess is deliberately silenced by the narrator in the gap which occurs at her confession, but the other gaps offer different complications in the novel. For example, the first gap not only stands in for Tess's rape, it also enables Hardy's narrator to gloss over the details of her time with Alec. Presumably Tess was something like a 'kept mistress' for Alec at this time. The page break enables Hardy's narrator to simply sum up these few weeks – in which Tess may've slept with Alec a number of times – as a daze for Tess ('"[m]y eyes were dazed by you for a little, and that was all"' XII).

Another break in the narrative occurs between chapter XIII and XIV, which's Tess's pregnancy. One can see how the description of Tess's pregnancy and childbirth would have not been possible in the serial of *Tess* in *Graphic* magazine, and not permissible in contemporary 1890s novels. However, this leap of months between chapters XIII and XIV misses out a hugely important experience in Tess's life. Instead, she is seen in a pose which echoes both the woman as worker and woman as mother, when she suckles her baby in an image redolent of thousands of *Virgin Mary with Child* paintings. The moments of crisis, of sex and death, are marginalized by the narrator.

The break between the second and third Phases is not as significant as the others. The break between the third and fourth Phases ('The Rally' and 'The Consequence') turns on an erotic moment, the kiss between Angel and Tess. The erotic nature of this break is echoed again, between the fifth Phase ('The Woman Pays') and the sixth ('The Convert'), when Tess sees Alec again after years. The narrative between these Phases (3rd and 4th, 5th and 6th) remains pretty much continuous. Between the fourth and fifth Phase is Tess's confession, discussed elsewhere, but a break between Phases that is over-shadowed by the two earlier important breaks occurs between the sixth Phase, 'The Convert', and the ironically titled 'Phase the Seventh: Fulfilment'. This gap depicts Tess's second, fatal fall, her return to Alec d'Urberville.

Much of 'Phase the Sixth: The Convert' depicts Alec's re-seduction of Tess. As before, Alec appears as a persistent personality who will not be put off taking Tess for himself again. What Hardy's narrator declines to depict, as before, is the actual moment in which this act of repossession occurs. Again, Hardy's narrator leads up to the reclamation carefully, describing in detail Tess's family's ignominious journey to Kingsbere. Marian and Izz are seen for the last time in the novel, on the journey. The last time Tess is seen directly by the reader, so to speak, before Angel sees her at the Sandbourne hotel, is in Kingsbere church. Here occurs the last of Alec's unsubtle joke appearances, as a knightly d'Urberville atop a tomb.

Thomas Hardy's narrator does not depict exactly how Tess agrees to leave her family and go with Alec to Sandbourne. The page break neatly excuses him from describing this critical moment. The reader is abandoned again, and has to supply the crucial details. For this is an *immense* change of direction for Tess: to have kept away from him for so long, then to give in and go to him. It's amazing, really. Does she 'have' to go? No. Is she 'forced' to? No. *Must* she go? No. Does she desire Alec? Better to say, does she desire love, to be loved? Yes. Angel recognizes what a passionate person she is ('for the first time Clare learnt what an impassioned woman's kisses were like', XXX).

The way the scene is played between Tess and Alec in Kingsbere church indicates how they will get on in their second time together: he jokes with her, while she sits next to the d'Urberville vaults and wishes she was with the dead. Alec makes a joke about the d'Urberville ancestry which has a distinctly bawdy overtone: '"[t]he little finger of the sham d'Urberville can do more for you than the whole dynasty underneath"' (LII). In Shakespearean drama Alec's 'little finger' would take on a phallic gloss. Again, sex is aligned with economics: the way out Alec offers Tess always has both – no money from him without sex.

How much Tess Durbeyfield herself is to 'blame' for what happens to her is indeed the heart of the novel. The reader has already seen, in the strawberry sequence, that Tess partly consciously accepts what Alec offers her, and as the strawberry scene looks directly forward to the rape scene, Tess can be seen as being partly complicit in her catastrophe.

The narrator emphasizes Tess's submissiveness, and many (male) critics have also seen Tess's passivity as her defining characteristic. Her 'passivity' is needed by the narrator in order to 'excuse' her from what happens to her. Whether it was rape or not, then, is crucial, because it reverberates throughout the novel. If it wasn't rape, then Tess's act of murder is wildly out of place. Alec, in short, does not 'deserve' such a fate, and such a drastic action is unnecessary. Even if Alec had raped her, Tess's act of murder is unforgivable in a so-called 'liberal', 'democratic' society. Tess's first act of 'revenge' for her rape, her confession to Angel, backfires dramatically. In the second act of 'revenge', she makes sure it'll work, by stabbing Alec herself. If Tess is not raped, but seduced, and is complicit in the act, then it's not clear what her motives are when she stays with Alec for the following few weeks. Even if she is raped, she stays far longer than one would expect her to, bearing in mind her character, and how she acts in the rest of the novel. The point is that *Tess of the d'Urbervilles* does not present a simple black and white case; this is why it is such a rich work. It would be too easy and obvious if Tess was raped and Alec was a total villain. It is precisely in those grey areas, on the margins between sex, desire, fear and need, that the novel is most interesting.

The narrator of *Tess of the d'Urbervilles* is ambivalent about the rape, which's partly what creates the confusions. Seen as having been 'mastered' by Alec, the act is seen as rape for Tess; but the narrator enfolds Tess with desire, so that 'insofar as priority is given to the narrator's erotic gratification at the re-emergence of Tess as image, Alec's action will assume the status of a seduction' commented Kaja Silverman (1984).

Can a country 'maiden' really be so 'innocent' of such things as intercourse? Hardy's narrator would have the reader believe so. However, this is not Tess's 'purity'. Tess takes in the strawberry half-willingly, and later possibly takes Alec into her body half-willingly. However, if the difference between seduction and rape is a question of degree, there is a world of difference between taking a strawberry and being raped, bearing a bastard child, being a single mother, seeing the child die and baptizing it. After eating the strawberry, Tess takes others, and goes about in a 'half-pleased, half-reluctant state'. This is also her state when she is in a 'daze' during the few weeks with Alec – not really enjoying herself, certainly not 'happy', but reluctant to leave because of the material comforts. *Tess*'s narrator is unsure about Tess's sexuality: is she a sensual, erotic woman, or, as Angel idealizes her, a fresh, pure, virginal woman?

Just after she's been raped Tess meets the religious texts man. Sure the scene is hardly subtle – Tess being confronted by the hypocrisy of Christian dogma: 'THY, DAMNATION, SLUMBERETH, NOT' and 'THOU, SHALT, NOT, COMMIT, ADULTERY'. This is sledgehammer storytelling, and Thomas Hardy knows it. It is another example of showing that, in Christianity, 'the letter killeth', which became central to the anti-religion polemic of *Jude the Obscure*. *Tess of the d'Urbervilles* explores and parodies the terrain of language and power (C. Thompson, 1983).

At this point in *Tess*, the social condemnation of Tess's behaviour implied in these dogmatic sayings from Judæo-Christianity is straightforward. What is more interesting about the scene is that Tess is being hounded by society directly. As the six week time with Alec is glossed over in the blank pages, what the reader sees is Tess going from being a 'maiden' to being a 'maiden no more' and having the conversation with Alec on her departure. A paragraph later, and the Biblical text man is with her. Soon they're having a theological discussion in the early Sunday morning in October. Just as Tess's mental landscape is 'blighted' by her rape, so the sign painter blights the countryside with his religious texts (C. Thompson, 1983). One man 'inscribes' his will and desire on her body, another man 'writes' his morality on the body of the Earth.

Curiously, Hardy's narrator has the text writer refer to each saying as 'tex', not 'text'. It seems as if Hardy's narrator is deliberately drawing attention to the affinities between 'tex' and 'sex'. A number of meanings may cluster around this emphasis. It's Tess's sex that is the pivot of much of the tragedy, or point, or theme, of the novel. The narrative explores the nexus Tess-tex-sex (and 'Wessex', in the term coined by a critic 'Wes-sexuality'). The two things, sex and text, are of course seen as a continuity in deconstruction and post-Derridan philosophy. Critics speak of the

129

'sexuality of the text' (Barthes' *jouissance*), but also of the 'textuality of sex' (Jacques Derrida, Paul de Man, J. Hillis Miller, Julia Kristeva). The 'sexuality' or *jouissance* of Hardy's texts is strident, and needs no explanation – humanist Hardy critics since the first Hardy reviews have been extolling it. The 'textuality of sex', though, and other postmodern/ cultural theory notions, have only been addressed by a few Hardy critics (Margaret Higonnet, Elizabeth Langland, Peter Widdowson, John Goode and others). Tess as 'sex' has been discussed by feminist critics of Hardy, in particular the relations between sex and gender, the relations between being female, femininity and feminism. This is as expected from 'second wave' feminism. Far less common are the studies of Tess as 'text'.

By calling the (religious) text a 'tex', the affinity is made by the narrator not only between 'tex' and 'sex' but also between 'text' and 'Tess'. Tess herself is indeed the 'text' of the novel, the surface upon which each character 'writes' their own version of Tess. Her mother 'writes' her as a beauty who might materially enrich the family – Joan Durbeyfield literally acts as a painter, dressing Tess up and standing back to admire her handiwork. Angel 'writes' Tess as a virginal, pure, poetic country maid.

Tess as the 'tex' of the novel is a text to be followed closely, or ignored, a 'tex'/ Tess to be exalted but not read closely (by Angel), to be loved for her surface beauty but ignored/ silenced (by Alec). As Helena Michie notes, Tess is a 'text to be read, interpreted, and edited by her two lovers' (112f). Both suitors see the surface Tess as a blemishless 'text' upon which they 'write' their own fantasies and projections. For Alec, Tess is a nebulous whiteness at his feet, passively waiting for him to make his mark of phallic lust upon her. For Angel Tess-tex is equally clad in virginal white, for he never shakes off that first sight of Tess in her white smock at the club-walking. As the epitome of 'virgin territory' for Angel, Tess must be as pure as an unwritten piece of blank paper, upon which he can inscribe his dreams. When he finds that someone has written over the virginal Tess-'tex', it's no wonder that Angel recoils in horror. Instead of purity he finds dirt, the white body has been blackened, and Tess's purity for Angel becomes abjected, in the Kristevan model.

As Julia Kristeva says of abjection, in her book *Powers of Horror*, it is the mud in Narcissus' pool, just what Narcissus would *not* like to find when he gazes erotically at himself. Kristevan abjection is what is neither inside nor outside, what is 'quite close but... cannot be assimilated. It beseeches, worries, and fascinates desire', is neither object nor subject, it destroys unity (J. Kristeva, 1982, 1-15).

Kristeva sees the artist's project as the purifying of abjection. This is what Angel has to do, but his religion does not equip him for such a task. Abjection lies behind the history of religions: the abject is simultaneously the 'land of oblivion' and that 'veiled infinity', the moment 'when revelation bursts forth' (ib., 9). The abject is the borderland of ambiguity, a total subjectivity. Ironically, it is *jouissance* that 'alone causes the abject to exist as such. One does not know it, one does not desire it, one joys in it [*on en jouit*]. Violently and painfully. A passion' (ib., 9). The abject, though, is not an object, not something that can be named, not something assimilable, not something definable.

The abject is not the Other, nor is it otherness; it is not, either, the subject's correlative. The only quality that the abject has is that it is opposed to the 'I', the subject. The abject worries and seduces desire; yet it cannot be assimilated, so desire rejects it. Even so, there is an impetus or spasm, a leap that is made 'towards an elsewhere as tempting as it is condemned' (ib., 1).

Tess's debasement later on in *Tess of the d'Urbervilles* is as nothing, in a way, compared with her self-humiliation at Angel's feet. It is disgusting to see Tess collapsing at Angel's feet and begging for forgiveness. The fault lies not entirely with Angel: Tess too is compounded by patriarchal lies and taboos. For the narrator, Angel is the weaker character: '[h]e looked upon her as a species of impostor; a guilty woman in the guise of an innocent one' (XXXV). Yet Tess's very body and presence makes the unspeakable – the rape – visible and unavoidable. While all those around her wish her to sweep it under the carpet, Tess's living presence makes the taboo painfully visible. She becomes a blot that must be eradicated. Her (sexually defiled) presence is too disruptive. In the end, society does get rid of it.

There is something in Tess that Alec and Angel do not see – her 'very self' (XXXV). Tess says '"I thought, Angel, that you loved me – me, my

131

very self"'. Alas, no, he does not see her very self.

Tess's sexually wounded presence exacerbates the ideological negation of women. *Tess of the d'Urbervilles* is a patriarchal text, despite its proto-feminism: Hardy was prevented by censorship from describing experiences such as pregnancy. Even mentioning pregnancy, let alone depicting it, was censored in Victorian times.[14] The feminism in *Tess of the d'Urbervilles* always makes concessions to the patriarchal, masculinist cultural climate of the late Victorian era. Hardy wanted to go further, depict even more harsh realities, but could not within the magazine market. Today, a hundred plus years later, there are still many things that cannot be shown – even things as harmless as an erection. A scene such as the killing of the live pig in *Jude the Obscure* could not be shown on film or TV these days. Blasting away people, in Hollywood movies such as *Terminator, Reservoir Dogs, The Wild Bunch* and *Rambo,* is acceptable, but not the killing of an innocent animal (even though people eat animals in their millions).

Forbidden to speak for so long, Tess Durbeyfield finally does speak: but her act of speaking destroys Angel's delicate constitution. There are few places where Tess is allowed to speak: the second is her letter to Angel; her third act of passionate speaking – to Alec, in her anger after meeting Angel in Sandbourne – goes unheeded. It is one of Tess's most passionate speeches:

> *...you had used your cruel persuasion upon me... you did not stop using it – no – you did not stop! ...and you taunted me... And at last I believed you and gave way! ...O, you have torn my life all to pieces...* (LVI)

It is then (and very quickly) that Tess decides to speak in a different way: to kill. 'Culture, at least patriarchal culture,' Luce Irigaray contends, 'would prohibit then the return to *red blood,* and even sex' (ib., 107). In Irigaray's reading of patriarchy, society suppresses real life, with its painful blood mysteries. Instead there are pseudo-feminine blood mysteries, such as the Mass and Eucharist. Or, in patriarchal mythology, a heroic blood-letting, such as war, which appropriates women's mysteries such as menstruation in a distinctly violent and masculine way.

When women take up such aggressive ideological positions, masculine society becomes very unsettled. Women hitting back at their male partners is still seen as unusual and as news in the contemporary world because it disrupts patriarchal norms. Focussing on women cutting off their husband's penises or murdering them covertly admits that women-beating is the norm. Men beating women is not seen as news or out-of-the-ordinary in Western patriarchal society. Viewed from a mainly Anglo-American feminist perspective, *Tess of the d'Urbervilles* records the suppression of red blood, feminine sex and wildness. The use of 'virile force' by men, as Marguerite Duras notes, reinforces the 'silence of women'.[15] In the end, Tess sees no alternative than to use men's means, the ones that have been used against her.

Tess's fourth act of speaking is when she tells Angel she has killed Alec:

> *I have done it... He had come between us and ruined us, and now he can never do it anymore. I never loved him at all, Angel, as I loved you... Why did you go away – why did you – when I loved you so? ...I could not bear the loss of you any longer – you don't know how entirely I was unable to bear your not loving me! Say you do now, dear, dear husband; say you do, now I have killed him!* (LVII)

Alec may not be as villainous as a conventional reading of *Tess of the d'Urbervilles* might suggest. There is evidence, critics have pointed out, that he actually loved Tess, and may even have loved her throughout the novel (unlike Angel); he offers to help Tess when she first leaves him, and when her husband has deserted her; he buys things for her family; he feels angry when Tess is working for Farmer Groby and is treated badly by her employer; Tess may even 'use' Alec to a certain extent, though he expects something in return. If Alec is not all bad (and he can't be, or Tess would have had nothing to do with him at all); then his death becomes unnecessary. If Alec had loved Tess continuously through the novel, his death is vastly out of proportion with the emotions in the narrative.

While Alec does what he likes (though he is a slave to (his) lust), Tess Durbeyfield labours in the fields. She has responsibilities – to her family, her parents and friends (M. Humm, 1995, 38). The men do not have to look after anybody, they are socially mobile. Alec gives up wandering as a preacher and rides his horse again, taking up the leisurely life of the financially well-off. Alec is not all bad, of course: there are men much worse in their sadism than Alec. One imagines that Hardy, if not constrained by Victorian values in magazine publishing, would have gone much further in depicting Alec's depravity. For D.H. Lawrence, Alec may be Tess's true 'mate': '[n]o ordinary man could have betrayed Tess', Lawrence reckons. [16] It was not so much Alec as the whole gender he was a part of that betrayed Tess. It was her ideals and hopes for life that were betrayed. It was not Alec who betrayed her, but all the people around her. Tess thought society was much better than that. She was also disappointed that a life could ruined by rape and unmarried motherhood. Sex shouldn't be able to ruin people. Indeed, it doesn't ruin Tess: she gets up, dusts herself off, and carries on living.

Angel is just as patronizing as Alec – he calls her 'child' and 'little thing'. Angel does not become violent with Tess, like Alec, but he does hit someone in the inn who insults her. Tess is not exceptional, the narrator says, and Thomas Hardy says this in his writings about the novel. Tess wants what society wants (and pressurizes) her to want: a man, a husband, a heterosexual, domestic life full of work and children. The novel severely criticizes these demands of society, as feminists do, and how they are manifested in the individual. What Hardy despises is the social law that demands 'you must be married' and then says 'don't come to us if it goes wrong'.

Society demands participation – not only in marriage, but in being sexual. Even if one isn't married, one must have a sexual life. Feminists have noted that hetero-patriarchy not only demands 'compulsory heterosexuality' (Adrienne Rich's phrase), but also compulsory sexuality. To negate sexuality, to be celibate or prefer not to deal with sexuality, is partly to be a non-person. Sexuality is such a large part of the construction of identity, in patriarchal societies, that people cannot understand it when others wish to subvert it. Thus, Alec cannot understand Tess not wanting to be in an erotic relationship with someone. Her husband absconding in Brazil, Tess simply wants to be left alone to get on with living. For Alec, this is madness, a waste of a life. There she is, with her soft body, which he must have.

Tess Durbeyfield regards Alec at times as her 'natural' husband – that is, as her true partner, sexually as well as socially. When she meets Angel in Sandbourne she says that the '"step back to him was not so great as it seems"', again emphasizing that she regarded her erotic relations with Alec as more fundamental, in the eyes of society, than her spiritual relationship with Angel. Angel too emphasizes the 'naturalness' of Alec being her husband: '"[h]ow can we live together while that man lives? – he being your husband in Nature, not I"' (XXXVI). Both Angel and Tess emphasize the importance for themselves of sexual relations: Angel in his reaction to Tess's rape, and Tess in regarding her rapist as her 'natural' husband. Through Tess and Angel society expresses the widespread significance of sex. Alec also uses the 'natural' argument, but couches it in moralist language: '"has not a sense of what is morally right and proper any weight with you?"' he asks Tess as he tries to persuade her to marry him (XLVI).

J. Hillis Miller asked questions of *Tess of the d'Urbervilles* such as, why is it that Tess is doomed to repeat the same event/s in her past and in the ancestral past, in her life, and other people's lives? (1982, 116) The continual questions of 'why?' that *Tess of the d'Urbervilles* raises at each point of crisis are the ones that readers ask of all Hardy's fiction. Why does Tess seem to be relatively immature or 'less shrewd and worldly-wise' than she might be expected to be? (A. Kettle, 54) Why doesn't she know about men and sex, when she lives in a lively rural community in which people would presumably have spoken frankly about sex? Also, with her group of same-age friends sex and boys would have been topics of conversation, as they supposedly are in young women's magazines such as *Sugar, Mizz, J-17,* and *Blis.* Why did Tess go to Trantridge, knowing what Alec's intentions probably were? Why didn't she try another job, and remain in Marlott? Why didn't she tell Angel about her past in another letter, when the first one was mislaid?

More questions: why didn't Angel turn back to find Tess after Izz had told him she would have done anything for him? (R. Morrell, 1965). He was 'within a featherweight's turn' of doing so. If Tess had told him of his sleepwalking, which she was on the point of doing, it might 'have prevented much misunderstanding and woe' (XXXVII). The night before, after he's been out wandering and wondering, Angel goes up to check on

Tess. He turns to leave her bedroom, then turns back again, as if to enter her room (and also to enter her body – it's their honeymoon night). But he catches sight of the d'Urberville portrait, which unsettles him (XXXV). There he is, outside her bedroom, on his wedding night, knowing underneath he really loves her, and knowing that she adores him, yet he doesn't go in. Scared off by a painting! What renunciation!

Many of these questions stem from Thomas Hardy's plots. Why the sudden passivity in characters? Why the unbelievable coincidences? Why the misunderstandings? Hardy's novels do not bear up to too much analysis in terms of plot, action and causality. In *Tess of the d'Urbervilles*, there are many moments when Hardy's plot stretches credibility. One is inclined to keep asking, as little Abraham does, '"[i]s it like that *really*, Tess?"' (I. iv)

Tess moves from an oral to a written culture, from folk ways to civilization, from speech to *écriture*. *Tess of the d'Urbervilles* describes 'the masculinzation of Tess's voice and the feminization of Angel's' (H, 24). But why did Tess wait so long before writing to Angel in South America? Or, more correctly, why did Hardy's narrator wait so long before including Tess's letters in the text? Angel had been having a terrible time in Brazil for months, so one of Tess's passionate letters (which he cherishes when they do arrive), would probably have changed his mind. Returning sooner to Wessex, Angel may have been re-united with Tess. His return was only a few weeks too late, but that's plenty in Hardy's erotic world. '"Too late, too late!"' says Tess mournfully (LV).

Why does Tess have to kill Alec? She could simply have left him. He was still in bed. She could have walked out of the door with Angel. She may have had a few belongings with her at the Sandbourne hotel, but nothing she would have minded leaving behind. Or she could have gone upstairs, dressed, said she was going out to buy something she needed, and left with Angel. On the way to Emminster, Tess would have been re-united with Angel, and his parents too would be reconciled with her and their son. They'd leave for a farm in the North of England. If Alec brought the case to court, he would probably lose, and anyway Tess could still leave him for Angel. And then, after killing Alec, why does Tess lose her sense of will and direction? Why does she not seem bothered about running away with Angel?

Instead there's the murder – again, significantly, not shown: Thomas Hardy's narrator is more concerned with the effect or impact of the murder, than the act itself. The murder means blood is spilt, and this is what is shown, coming through the ceiling. Significantly, language again plays a key role in the murder sequence: Alec calls Tess's beloved a 'foul name' and this is partly what drives her to murder him – literally, to shut him up. Similarly, when Jude is weak and seemingly incapable of sudden direct action, he leaps up to pin Arabella down when she calls Sue a hussy. Having been silenced herself, by a host of social, psychological and cultural factors, Tess finally manages to silence her pursuer – to have, as far as *she's* concerned, the last word. At the beginning of the novel, he forced the strawberry (phallic object) in her mouth, now she thrusts back the phallic object, the knife.

Tess of the d'Urbervilles is probably the most accomplished example of Hardy's union of the concerns of class, labour, materialism, sexual politics and social status. *Tess of the d'Urbervilles* brilliantly exposes the hypocrisies found in the notions of inherited and earnt rank, in labour and economy, in property and ownership. Hardy ruthlessly highlights the brutality inherent in these problematical areas of the human condition. Alec's gift to Tess Durbeyfield is sex and materialist wealth. He buys her disinherited family a horse; he gives Tess a kind of home in the Sandbourne hotel. Angel gives her spirituality, but nothing materially. Alec, though a false aristocrat, is practical. Angel, more noble, is impractical. His Brazilian escapade goes terribly wrong. John Durbeyfield finds out he is a descendant of a titled and prestigious county family, but he is not able to do anything with this knowledge. Joan Durbeyfield is more practical. She sends Tess away, but also withholds important information from her daughter about sex and men's predatory nature.

Tess of the d'Urbervilles is not only a great novel of the tensions between nature, sexuality, character and spirituality, it also engages face-on the vicissitudes of class, labour, wealth, knowledge and economic politics. Thomas Hardy's Wessex is not only a world of nature, emotion, personality and the spirit of place (the Hardy of the romantic 'heritage' novel, beloved of BBC serialization), it is also a world of great social change, in which the ideological forces at work are changing rapidly. The working class figures – Marty, Oak, Tess, Jude – try to cling on to the old ways of earning a living. Tess and Marty carry on working in the way they have always done. But they are overtaken by a new group of controllers, who have new methods. The way that Tess and Jude try to earn a living is far below what they are capable of doing.

Tess Durbeyfield is one of the great survivors of literature, even though she dies. One of the amazing things about *Tess of the d'Urbervilles* is that it involves the death of the heroine – after she has already been raped (J. Goode, 1988, 137). Yet *Tess of the d'Urbervilles* remains a life-affirming text. Despite the many mistakes, confusions, backtrackings and failures, and the narrator's sometimes gleeful dwelling on them, *Tess of the d'Urbervilles* is an inspiring text. Tess impresses because, as D.H. Lawrence writes, she 'never tries to alter or to change anybody... She respects utterly the other's right to be' (*Study*, 95).

Tess is not a 'feminine' text in the Cixous manner, nor does it articulate the Kristevan *chora* like *avant garde* modernist writing. *Tess* is not the expression, either, of the two lips speaking together of Luce Irigaray, nor is it the articulation of the female 'wild zone' of Elaine Showalter. It is, however, a novel of rage and oppression which feminists such as Andrea Dworkin, Adrienne Rich, Alice Walker and Susan Griffin might applaud. Despite being a feminist or proto-feminist novel, *Tess of the d'Urbervilles* is popular with critics partly because it flatters and reflects their views. *Tess* has been popular with male critics because there is plenty in it that does not severely challenge their masculinist, patriarchal views and ideologies. If *Tess of the d'Urbervilles* were an openly radical feminist text, it would probably not have achieved its status as one of the most discussed books in literature. Very few aggressively feminist books become 'classics'. *Tess of the d'Urbervilles* is also successful because it does everything a good novel should do: it has a strong story and settings, powerfully rendered characters, 'great' themes, and so on. *Tess* is successful too because the reader is invited to identify wholly with the heroine, in the classic way of the Hollywood film.[17]

VIII

Marriage and Feminism
in *Jude the Obscure*

Jude the Obscure is a sister (or brother) novel to *Tess of the d'Urbervilles*. The author attacks similar targets: the family, homelife, politics, religion, marriage, education and sexuality. *Jude the Obscure*, though, contains far more polemic and philosophizing than *Tess* or any of the earlier novels. The preaching and polemic threatens to undo the narrative, which is nevertheless 'realist', like other Thomas Hardy fictions. In *Jude the Obscure*, Hardy was stretching the novel to the limit, testing the boundaries of what is 'acceptable'. In *Jude the Obscure*, the things that say 'you shan't' are, variously, God, religion, society, education, circumstance, chance, nature, and marriage. All of these institutions and 'causes' reside inside the individual, which is what makes the problems they create so difficult to deal with for Sue and Jude. Patriarchy, culture and society are not in some 'out there' space, but inside people.

Marriage is the battleground here.[1] The discourse of marriage dominates *Jude the Obscure*. Every time Sue Bridehead and Arabella meet without Jude (in Aldbrickham, and at the Kennetbridge fair) the subject is marriage; at the Great Agricultural Show, the overriding discourse is Arabella's musings on the Sue-Jude marriage; when Arabella meets her friend Anny at the Show Anny tells her she is soon going to be married (V. v). It seems there is no other subject worthy of discussion in the middle sections of *Jude the Obscure*. Every character relies on it for fulfilment. Sue and Phillotson have teaching to consider, but when Sue leaves Phillotson, his life decays rapidly. Jude only prospers, emotionally as well as materially, when he is with Sue. Secondary characters such as Widow Edlin and Gillingham further emphasize the centrality of the marital discourse.

Widow Edlin's opinion is important – it is not, like Gillingham's or Arabella's, on any particular 'side' in the central tangle of desire. Mrs Edlin's advice is common sense and plain-speaking. '"You are in love wi' t' other still! ...You be t' other man's"' says Widow Edlin (VI. v). Sue knows it in herself but won't admit it to others. Mrs Edlin even commends Sue and Jude for trying to live without marrying, that is, trying not to make the same mistake twice. Widow Edlin intercedes practically at one point, when she tries to persuade Phillotson to delay the wedding.

Their 'experiment' fails. '"Perhaps the world is not illuminated enough for such experiments as ours!"' Sue Bridehead muses (VI. iii). Sue and Jude are described as being fifty years ahead of their time (V. iv). It's not *their* fault, Sue says, but society's – that it is backward, and can't keep up with them. Why can't society see, Sue says, that for such as us matrimony is 'the most preposterous of all joint-ventures' (V. iv). In the 'experiment' in erotic relationship of Sue and Jude, and in other relationships, Hardy was, according to a critic, 'telling his contemporaries that they had not yet imagined the human consequences of honestly living out the modernist premises' (D. De Laura, 1967).

Jude the Obscure is cyclical – the events go round and round but get nowhere. There is no finale, no climax, no endpoint. Each 'marriage' is supplanted by another one. Situations repeat, with no possibility of escape. The final marriage is no consummation of the narrative, as in traditional stories, for there is a simultaneous funeral.[2] The narrator's statement after the eleven year-old 'natural boy' Jude has been beaten by Farmer Troutham sets the tone for the novel:

> *Growing up brought responsibilities, he found. Events did not rhyme quite as he had thought. Nature's logic was too horrid for him to care for.* (I. ii)

The scenes where Sue and Jude try to get married are suitably grim – but it's standard to regard registry office weddings as lacking in 'poetry' (V. iv). The imagery of the sullen, reluctant soldier and his pregnant, battered bride is suitably sordid (V. iv); but even the middle class church wedding the lovers observe nearby doesn't console Sue. She comes out with a striking image of ancient blood sacrifice which D.H. Lawrence would have approved: '"[t]he flowers in the bride's hand are sadly like the garland which decked the heifers of sacrifice in old times"' (V. iv). Sue's harsh sacrifical analogy is echoed ironically later on, when she goes back to Phillotson. As the narrator dryly calls it: 'the self-sacrifice of the woman on the altar of what she was pleased to call her principles' (VI. v).

At times all the fuss about getting married in Thomas Hardy's fiction – about 'putting up the banns', arranging licences, dreading the wedding day, rehearsing the occasion beforehand and capitulating at the last moment – can seem excessive. After all, in the XXIst century one can get married in Las Vegas with just an hour's notice. The marriage laws of the 19th century of course favoured men greatly. Phillotson would have been able to divorce Sue 'on the most facile of grounds' (R. Morgan, 1988, 135). Sue, though, according to the 1857 Statute, would have had to produce evidence that her husband had committed adultery, bigamy with adultery, adultery with desertion, sodomy, bestiality, or rape.

Neoplatonic ethereal love is fine until someone comes along and steals your man. When Arabella reappears at Aldbrickham, Sue goes into an apoplexy of sexual jealousy. '"Don't go now, Jude!... Don't, don't go, dear!... Don't! Please stay at home, Jude, and not go to her"' (V. ii). Again, the intensity of Sue's sexual envy shows just how important sex is to her. Sue would jump out of a window for the wrong man at the wrong time. '"It is torture to me to live with him as a husband!"' she tells Jude (IV. ii).

141

Both Arabella and Gillingham tell Phillotson that a wife shakes down after a few years to marriage. Indeed, Arabella advocates that men 'chain on' women and treat them roughly (V. viii).

Thomas Hardy's basic point is that marriage can become a prison which traps people who should part. As he explains in his 1912 *Postscript* to the 1895 *Preface*, 'a marriage should be dissolvable as soon as it becomes a cruelty to either of the parties' (xxxvii). This laudable humane vision forms the centre of the book, but the view is often expressed vehemently. In the *Preface*, Hardy calls *Jude the Obscure* 'simply an endeavour to give shape to a series of seemings, or personal impressions' (xxxv-xxxvi). Often, the 'series of seemings' becomes an argument or tract.[3] *Jude the Obscure* is at times a soap box tantrum, which mars it, according to some critics, such as Virginia Woolf.[4] As with *Tess*, the main theme of *Jude* is intolerance and inhumanity, part of Hardy's 'long plea against man's inhumanity to man – to woman – and to the lower animals' as he explained in a 1904 conversation (F. Pinion, 1968, 178).

Thomas Hardy contrasts the secret compact between lovers, as found in occultism, courtly love poetry, the *Song of Songs* and other (often heretical) cults or movements with the public, legal, religious institution of wedlock. What should be a personal bond of 'hand-fasting' between consenting adults is turned, in Hardy's view, into a constricting, dogmatic socio-religious edifice.

The 'immortal puzzle', as Hardy puts it in the *Preface* of *The Woodlanders*, is how to find a basis for the sexual relations between men and women (39). The 'immortal' sexual question is posed in *Jude the Obscure* by Sue Bridehead. If someone is suffering in a marriage, she tells her husband Phillotson, they should be able to be set free. For Sue, marriage is a 'horrible and sordid' undertaking. If the anti-marital tendencies in *Tess of the d'Urbervilles* had been proto-feminist, in *Jude the Obscure* they were directly and at times aggressively feminist. Sue's language is distinctly vehement: 'horrible and sordid'. No equivocation from her – though at other times she is less convinced by her thinking. For Sue, marriage is legitimised oppression and suppression, views with concord not only with mainly Anglo-American second wave feminism,[5] but also with postmodern feminism, as well as gay, queer and lesbian cultural theory. Sue articulates the oppressions of what gay theory calls 'hetero hell', where heterosexual couples are derisorily termed 'breeders', people whose function is to breed more people.

The intimate, secret feelings between two people become hardened into dogma and law: this is Hardy's polemic in *Jude the Obscure*. Passion becomes institutionalized. In the *Preface* to the novel he wrote of the 'fret and fever, derision and disaster' that can follow 'in the wake of the strongest passion known to humanity'; the aim of his novel, he said, was to 'tell, without a mincing of words, of a deadly war waged between flesh and spirit' (xxxv).

In Thomas Hardy's fiction, getting married can be a disaster of huge social, moral, religious and personal proportions. Listen to the language he uses to describe *Jude the Obscure*: 'disaster', 'strongest passion', 'deadly war', 'tragedy'. It is vivid, even apocalyptic language.

The tragedy of Sue and Jude is that there is no social or cultural space in which their special, two-in-one spiritual love can exist, let alone flourish. Their kind of loving is in fact tabooed by society: Hardy underlines the taboo by having them cousins, clearly evoking sister-brother incest, a feature of ancient Egyptian religion (in Isis and Osiris, Cleopatra and Ptolemy), and in esoteric movements such as Gnosticism, Neoplatonism and alchemy (the marriage of sun/ moon, silver/ gold, Venus/ Mars and King/ Queen).

Sue and Jude recall at times the mythical lovers of old (of course, Hardy would glow at the comparisons): Antony and Cleopatra, Héloïse and Abélard, Tristan and Isolde, Lancelot and Guinevere, Dante and Beatrice. Like so many lovers in fiction, Sue and Jude live their lives through the other person, as Cathy and Heathcliff do in *Wuthering Heights*. The cousin-relationship underlines the identity between the two lovers; when Sue dresses in Jude's clothes, she seems like a version of himself. In the manuscript of the novel, at the end of chapter three of Part Three, in a sentence that doesn't appear in subsequent editions, Jude sees in Sue 'as it were the rough material called himself done into another sex – idealized, softened, and purified' (440). The Melchester scene evokes crossdressing and Sue's playing with gender.

Thomas Hardy said he was 'more interested in this Sue story' than in any others he'd written.[6] Hardy exchanged some key letters about *Jude the Obscure* with his friend Edmund Gosse. Gosse in a review of *Jude* pinpointed Sue's sexual life as 'the central interest in the book'.[7] On the construction of *Jude the Obscure*, Hardy wrote to Gosse:

> ...*there is nothing perverted or depraved in Sue's nature. The abnormalism consists in disproportion, not in inversion, her sexual instinct being healthy as far as it goes, but unusually weak and fastidious. Her sensibilities remain painfully alert notwithstanding, as they do in nature with such women. One point illustrating this I could not dwell upon: that, though she has children, her intimacies with Jude have never been more than occasional, even when they were living together. (I mention that they occupy separate rooms, except towards the end), and one of her reasons for fearing the marriage ceremony is that she fears it would be breaking faith with Jude to withhold herself at pleasure, or altogether, after it; though while uncontracted she feels at liberty to yield herself as seldom as she chooses. This has tended to keep his passion as lust at the end as at the beginning, and helps to break his heart. He has never really possessed her as freely as he desired.*[8]

Thomas Hardy's explanation or apology of *Jude the Obscure* reveals some interesting points. Firstly, one sees that Hardy's narrator puts much of the 'blame' of the tragedy of the novel onto Sue. This is sometimes unconsciously done, for Hardy consciously exalts Sue. But he can't disguise the undercurrent of his opinion, namely that Sue's fastidiousness or 'weak' sexual appetite is partly to blame for the ensuing tragedy. It is not Jude's sexuality that is at fault. He is simply healthily lustful, which Hardy's narrator (and Sue) regards as 'normal'. Sue tells that Jude that his 'wickedness', his lust for her, was only 'the natural desire to possess the woman' (VI. iii). Sue thus condones the sexual predatory nature of men. Sue says of Jude that it is not sexual desire in itself that is 'wrong'.

What anti-censorship feminists say of pornography is pertinent here: Avedon Carol and Nettie Pollard maintain:

> *it is the fact that men feel entitled to make these demands which is disgusting – not what they desire sexually. This is not caused by depictions of sex acts in pornography, but by a sexist society that does not afford women full human or sexual status.*[9]

Sue is willing to continue to live as Platonic lovers, 'in mental communion'. Jude objects, saying that '"people could not live for ever like that"'. Jude seems to mean 'men' more than 'people' here, and Sue immediately replies: '"[w]omen could: men can't, because they – won't."' (VI. iii) Concerning sleeping with Phillotson, Sue says she has 'a personal feeling against it – a physical objection – a fastidiousness' (IV. ii). Sue's 'weak' sexual hunger, however, places her outside of the sexual norms, and causes the disruption in the Sue-Jude relationship. Sue simply won't fuck as much as Jude – or Phillotson – would like.

Marriage is sanctified rape, said the 1970s radical feminists. An extreme view, perhaps, but Sue is aware of it, eighty years earlier, in the 1890s, when she says marriage is like being licensed to be loved on the premises (V. i). For Sue, as for radical feminists such as Andrea Dworkin, Susan Griffin, Kate Millett and Mary Daly, marriage legitimizes the man's desire for sex. He must fuck her whenever he likes. The wife must always be available to him.

This feminist view of marriage and sex is backed up by an examination of the rape and marital laws from mediæval times onwards. Rape within marriage was not acknowledged: it was the woman's 'duty' to give herself up sexually to the man. It was not his desire that was seen as 'abnormal', but her partner's desire to withhold herself. Fucking is 'normal', and the desire to transcend fucking was regarded with suspicion in mediæval and Renaissance times.

One sees this suspicion in the plays of Shakespeare, where characters are jeered at if they choose to go beyond sex. Celibacy becomes laughable from Shakespeare onwards in Western culture. You must put your genitals somewhere, is the socio-sexual assumption. You must live somewhere, you must eat something, you must have desires. One must fuck, is the assumption. It's the norm. A similar abhorrence of 'abnormal' behaviour occurs when people stress that they don't drink, or don't smoke. *What? You don't drink? What* are *your 'vices' or luxuries, then?* Everyone, it is assumed in patriarchal culture, must love sex, and have sex, or cigarettes, or drinking, or drugs, or some 'vice' or 'luxury'.

In his letter to Edmund Gosse, Thomas Hardy says that he was restrained by censorship from detailing the sexual aspects of the Sue-Jude relationship. And in "Candour in English Fiction" he complains about being censored, so that *Jude* was partly conceived as a way of destroying the taboo on 'those issues which are not to be mentioned in respectable magazines and select libraries' (Per, 130). One wonders what Hardy would have written if he had not cared a jot about censorship or publication (critics cite Lawrence's *The Rainbow* as an example of what Hardy might have written).[10] Or if Hardy had written the novel post-1960, after the vindication of *Lady Chatterley's Lover*, perhaps there would have been detailed sex scenes? One might have read about Jude Fawley going down on Sue Bridehead, and she pushing his head away from her clitoris, sighing, 'I just can't come today. Sorry.' We might have seen Jude badgering Sue for just one more blowjob.

Thomas Hardy shows in *Jude the Obscure* that one doesn't need genital details to portray the ravages of sexual relationships. One doesn't need to describe cocks and cunts, as D.H. Lawrence did, or dildoes and fist-fucking, as lesbian porn has done. The horror and revulsion, the desire and intensity of sex, is all there in Thomas Hardy's novels, without requiring the prose of soft (or hard) core pornography. It's an odd thing about literature, too, that Hardy was allowed by the socio-political climate of the late 19th century to describe in detail a young boy murdering two children then hanging himself, but could not describe the sexual relations between two adults. These curious double standards still apply to the media, where footage of death and destruction can be shown on the TV news, but scenes of 'sexual explicitness' are carefully policed. Death, but not sex; physical violence, but not physical love.

The most ironic – perhaps 'tragic' – aspect of *Jude the Obscure* is that both Sue Bridehead and Jude Fawley make the same mistake *twice*, they both marry the wrong person *twice*. As if once wasn't enough, as if once hadn't taught them *anything*. To make a mistake of such grand proportions once, but *twice*? It is upon this deeply ironic act that the 'tragedy' of *Jude the Obscure* is founded. Both Sue and Jude are thus martyrs – not only martyrs to society, in society, because of society – but martyrs to themselves. Sue and Jude are martyrs to their own skewed notions of morality, to their strange, neurotic temperaments, to their misperceptions of social realities.

It seems as if Sue is the changeable personality – at least, from Jude's point of view she's fickle. Sometimes she's a New Woman, or a liberated thinker, or someone strangely superstitious about religion and marriage. However, Jude's sexual personality is equally in flux, as the whole novel is in flux. For Jude, and for Phillotson, masculine (sexual) identity is not a fixed, constant entity; sometimes Jude is a youth, overcome by erotic desire which swamps other thoughts (as when he first meets Arabella); at other times he is an abstemious would-be priest. Part of the socio-sexual confusions of *Jude the Obscure* surround not only Sue but also Jude and Phillotson: their (sexual) masculinity is under attack.

As is clear from the men's fate, masculinity is also seen as a social and cultural construct, with limiting and damaging qualities. Indeed, much is made of Phillotson allowing Sue to leave him for her lover, Jude. The populace of Shaston cannot understand Phillotson letting his wife go, though they are not surprised that she leads him a merry dance. The narrator emphasizes the heterodox nature of Phillotson's act, which he sees as an act of mercy. Phillotson, then, also contributes towards the questioning of sexual politics in *Jude the Obscure*, as well as the lovers.

The sexual politics of *Jude the Obscure*, like other Thomas Hardy novels, does not step outside of traditional heteropatriarchy. Hardy conceives of the opposites or alternatives in his sexual politics as being 'man' or 'woman', masculine or feminine. The third alternative – of the lesbian or (more correctly) the lesbian feminist cultural position – is not considered in depth by Hardy or any of the main Victorian authors. Alternative sexual identities, such as lesbian, gay and queer, hardly figure in a sexual politics dominated by two-term heterosexual logic.

But you can bet that had Thomas Hardy been writing in an era of openly gay and lesbian communities – the 1980s or 1990s, say – he would surely have included openly gay and lesbian characters in his texts, and tackled gay and lesbian issues and themes.

NOTES

I   Introduction

1. J. Hillis Miller: "Steven's Rock and Criticism as Cure, II", *Georgia Review*, 30, 1976.

2. Hélène Cixous: *Jours de l'an [First days of the year],* 1990, in H. Cixous, 1994, 185.

3. F.R. Leavis: "Hardy the Poet", *Southern Review*, 1940; *The Great Tradition*, London, 1948.

4. Patricia Stubbs, for example, writes that Hardy is 'almost unique in the English nineteenth-century novel, in that he creates women who are sexually exciting' (1979, 65).

II   Thomas Hardy and Feminism

1. Peter Widdowson writes:

Hardy, as we have him, is so inscribed with the processes of the consumption and reproduction of his work in history that it is now, as it were, a palimpsest of the perceptions, evaluations, readings, re-readings, and rewritings of a particular literary and æsthetic – not to say national – tradition. (1989, 57)

2. Sarah Kozloff: "Narrative Theory", in R. Allen: *Channels of Discourse,* Methuen, 1987, 55.

3. Most Hardy criticism is distinctly patriarchal, it is 'based on a reading determined by a dominant gender ideology', and there's no doubting that this bias is masculine (George Wotton, 183).

4. Donald Hall, "Afterword", *Tess of the d'Urbervilles,* Signet, New

York, NY, 1964, 424.

5. Judith Mitchell: "Hardy's Female Reader", in H, 178.

6. Robert Kiely: "The Menace of Solitude: The Politics and Aesthetics of Exclusion in *The Woodlanders*", in H, 188.

7. Luce Irigaray: "Sexual Difference", in T. Moi, 1987, 124.

8. Judith Halberstam: "F2M: The Making of Female Masculinity", in L. Doan, 1994, 212.

9. Sue Wilkinson & Celia Kitzinger; "Dire Straights?: Contemporary Rehabilitation of Heterosexuality", in G. Griffin, 1994, 84

10. Catherine MacKinnon: "Feminism, Marxism, Method, and the State: An Agenda for Theory", in N.O. Keohane, ed. *Feminist Theory: A Critique of Ideology*, Harvester, 1982.

11. Critics such as A.O. Cockshut remain adamant: '[t]he attempt to turn Hardy into a feminist is altogether vain' (*Man and Woman: Love in the Novel 1740-1940*, Collins 1977, 129).

12. The sexual relations in Hardy's fiction, as in all fiction, occur within heteropatriarchal ideology. As Elizabeth Grosz writes, '[a]ll sexual practices… are made possible and function within the constraints of heterosexism and phallocentrism', but these are not perfect, immutable systems, Grosz asserts, 'they are contradictory systems, fraught with complexities, ambiguities, and vulnerabilities that can and should be used to strategically discern significant sites of contestation' ("Refiguring Lesbian Desire", in L. Doan, 1994, 69). Adrienne Rich, in "Compulsory Heterosexuality and Lesbian Existence", writes that 'gender inequality' also means 'the enforcement of heterosexuality for women as a means of assuring male right of physical, economical and emotional access' (1980).

13. Edwin Ardener: "Belief and the Problem of Women", in Shirley Ardener, ed. *Perceiving Women*, Halsted Press, New York, NY, 1978.

14. H. Cixous, "The Laugh of the Medusa", in E. Marks, 254.

15. Elaine Showalter writes:

We can think of the "wild zone" of women's culture spatially, experientially, or metaphysically. Spatially, it stands for an area which is literally no-man's land, a place forbidden to men… Experientially it stands for the aspects of the female life-style which are outside of and unlike those of men; again, there is a corresponding zone of male experience alien to women. But if we think of the wild zone metaphysically or in terms of consciousness, it has no corresponding male space since all of male consciousness is within the circle of the dominant structure and thus accessible to or structured by language.

Elaine Showalter: "Feminist Criticism in the Wilderness", in E. Showalter, 1986, 262-3; Jeanne Addison Roberts: *The Shakespearean Wild: Geography, Genus and Gender*, University of Nebraska Press, Lincoln, Nebraska, 1991, 1-5.

16. Sherry B. Ortner: "Is female to male as nature is to culture?", in M. Rosaldo & L. Lamphere, eds. *Woman, Culture and Society*, Stanford University Press, 1974.

17. Ann Rosalind Jones: "Writing the Body: L'Écriture féminine", in E. Showalter, 1986, 363.

18. Victor Burgin: "Geometry and Abjection", in J. Fletcher, 1990, 115-6.

19. L. Irigaray: *Ce sexe qui n'en est pas un*, Minuit, Paris, 1977, 28-29.

20. Luce Irigaray: "La différence sexuelle", *Ethiope de la différence sexuelle*, Minuit, Paris, 1984, and in Toril Moi, 1988, 128.

21. Moira Gatens: "Power, Bodies and Difference", in T. Barrett, 1992, 134.

22. J. Kristeva: "La femme, ce n'est jamais ça", *Tel Quel*, Autumn, 1974, in E. Marks, 135.

23. Hélène Cixous: "Sorties", in E. Marks, 95.

24. J. Kristeva: *About Chinese Women*, Marion Boyars, 1977, 63.

25. M. Duras, interview in *Signs*, Winter, 1975, in E. Marks, 175.

26. H. Cixous: "The Laugh of the Medusa", *Signs*, Summer, 1976, in E. Marks, 249.

27. Rachel DuPlessis: "For the Etruscans", in E. Showalter, 1986, 273.

28. Mary Jacobus: "Is There a Woman in This Text?", in *New Literary Criticism*, Autumn, 1982, 14, 1.

29. G. Spivak, 1990, 109. Emma Pérez: "Irigaray's Female Symbolic in the Making of Chicana Lesbian *Sitios y Lenguas (Sites and Discourses)*", in L. Doan, 108.

30. T. Moi: *Sexual/ Textual Politics*, 139.

31. See Susan Rubin Suleiman: "(Re)Writing the Body: The Politics of Female Eroticism", in *Risking Who One Is*, MIT Press, 1995, 14f; Elizabeth Grosz: "Desire, the body and recent French feminism', *Intervention*, 21-2, 1988, 28-33; Alison M. Jagger & Susan R. Bordo, eds. *Gender/ Body/ Knowledge: feminist reconstructions of being and knowing*, Rutgers University Press, New Brunswick, 1989; Naomi Schor: *Breaking the Chain: Women, Theory and French Realist Fiction*, New York, NY, 1985; and "This essentialism which is not one: coming to grips with Irigaray", *differences*, 1, 2, 1989.

32. Monique Witting: "One Is Not Born a Woman", speech at the Feminist as Scholar Conference, May, 1979, Barnard College, New York.

33. The phrases come from C. Schwichenberg: *The Madonna Connection: Representational Politics, Subcultural Identities and Cultural Theory*, Westview Press, Boulder, CO, 1993; R. Braidotti, *Patterns of Dissonance*, Polity, 1991; see L. Butler, 1990; S. Wilkinson in G. Griffin, 1994.

34. Becky Rosa sees monogamy as an ideology which society encourages women to conform to by using 'cultural products (the media), economic restraints (tax incentives, the high cost of single living), social factors (the provision of support and companionship, or social status and privilege) and by the notion that this is 'how it is', 'this is natural'' (B.

Rosa, in G. Griffin, 1994, 107-8).

35. Chritobel Mackenzie: "The Anti-Sexism Campaign Invites You to Fight Sexism, Not Sex", in A. Assiter, 1993, 144.

36. John Kucich: "Moral Authority in the Late Novel: The Gendering of Art", in H, 234; P. Stubbs, 1981, 58f; P. Boumelha, 1982, 48.

37. See Julia Kristeva: *Desire in Language; Révolution du language poétique*, Seuil, Paris, 1974.

38. Marxist-Feminist Literature Collective: "Women's Writing: *Jane Eyre, Shirley, Villette, Aurora Leigh*", in Francis Barker *et al*, eds. *1848: The Sociology of Literature*, in M. Eagleton, ed. *Feminist Literary Theory: A Reader*, 1979.

39. J. Kristeva: *Women's Time*, in *The Kristeva Reader*, 208.

40. J. Kristeva: *Histoires d'amour*, Denoël, Paris, 1983, and in *The Kristeva Reader*, 242.

41. J. Kristeva: *Women's Time*, in *The Kristeva Reader*, 191.

42. Christian Metz, "The Imaginary Signifier", *Screen*, 16, 2, Summer, 1975.

43. L.Irigaray: "The poverty of psychoanalysis", *The Irigaray Reader*, 101.

44. Helena Michie makes this point in relation to Pierston in *The Well-Beloved*, in *The Flesh Made Word: Female Figures and Women's Bodies*, Oxford University Press 1987, 112.

45. Luce Irigaray: *Speculum of the Other Woman*, tr. Gillian C. Gill, and *This Sex Which Is Not One*, tr. Catherine Porter, both Cornell University Press, New York, NY, 1985; see also: Dorothy Leland: "Lacanian psychoanalysis and French feminism: toward an adequate political psychology", *Hypatia*, 3, 3, Winter, 1989, 81-103.

46. Elizabeth Grosz: "Refiguring Lesbian Desire", in L. Doan, 75.

47. R.Rilke, letter to Clara Rilke, 8 March, 1907, in *Gesammalte Briefe 1892-1926*, Insel Verlag, Leipzig, 1940, II, 279f.

48. J. Lacan, "The meaning of the phallus", 1988; Bernard Baas: "Le désir pur", *Ornicar?*, 83, 1987.

49. C. Jung: *The Development of Personality*, vol. 17, Routledge, 1954, 198; Marie-Louise von Franz: *The Psychological Meaning of Redemption Motifs in Fairy Tales*, Inner City Books, Toronto 1980, 39f.

50. Emma Jung & Marie-Louise von Franz: *The Grail Legend, tr.* Andrea Dykes, Sigo Press, Boston, Mass., 1980, 64.

51. Larysa Mykyta: "Lacan, Literature and the Look", *SubStance*, 39, 1983, 54.

52. Lady Jayne ad, *Clothes Show* magazine, December, 1992.

53. See Laura Mulvey: "Visual pleasure and narrative cinema", *Screen*, 16, 3, 1975, 6-19.

54. Kristin Brady: "Textual Hysteria: Hardy's Narrator on Women", in H, 1993, 89.

55. Catherine King: "The Politics of Representation: A Democracy of the

Gaze", in F. Bonner, 136.

56. Luce Irigaray, "Women's Exile", in D. Cameron, 1990, 83; and Luce Irigaray, *Speculum.*

57. Dianne Fallon Sadoff: "Looking at Tess: The Female Figure in Two Narrative Media", in H, 151.

58. Emma Pérez: "Irigaray's Female Symbolic in the Making of Chicana Lesbian *Sitios y Lenguas (Sites and Discourses)*", in L. Doan, 108.

59. L. Irigaray: *Ce sexe qui n'en est pas un*, in E. Marks, 1981, 107.

60. M. Wynne-Davies, in V. Wayne.

61. J.E. Howard & M.F. O'Connor, ed. *Shakespeare Reproduced: The Text in History and Ideology*, Methuen, London, 1987.

62. Kristeva: "La femme, ce n'est jamais ça", *Tel Quel*, Autumn, 1974, in E. Marks, 135.

63. V. Traub, in V. Wayne.

III   Love, Sex and Marriage in Thomas Hardy's Fiction

1. Hardy's letter to Alexander Macmillan, 25 July 1868, in M. Seymour-Smith, 1995, 85.

2. Sappho, in *Greek Lyric Poetry*, ed. W. Barnstone, Schocken Books, New York, NY, 1977, 4.

3. J. Keats, 'Ode to Melancholy', *Poems*, Oxford, 1909, 141.

4. P. Shelley, *Selected Poems*, Dent, 1983, 163.

5. Stendhal, *De l'Amour*, Penguin, 1975.

6. J. Kristeva: "In Praise of Love", in *Tales of Love*, 6.

7. Paul Éluard wrote:

La vie sans cesse a recherche d'un novel amour, par effacer l'amour ancient, l'amour dangereux, la vie voulait changer d'amour. [Life unceasingly searching for a new love, to obliterate the old love, the dangerous love, life wanted to change love.] (From *Uninterrupted Poetry*, New Directions, New York, NY, 1975, 22-23.)

8. Hélène Cixous: "Extreme Fidelity", in S. Sellers, 1988, and in H. Cixous, 1994, 132.

9. H. Cixous, *(With) Ou l'art de l'innocence [(With) Or the art of innocence]*, 1981, in H. Cixous, 1994, 95.

10. Kristin Brady: "Textual Hysteria: Hardy's Narrator on Women", in H, 1993, 94.

11. In her essay "Refiguring Lesbian Desire", Elizabeth Grosz describes desire in post-Lacanian/ Hegelian terms which accords with desire in Hardy's fiction:

The only object desire can desire is an object that will not fill the lack or provide complete satisfaction. To provide desire with its object is to annihilate it. Desire desires to be desired. Thus, for Hegel, the only object that both satisfies desire yet perpetuates it is not an object but another desire... Desire is the movement of substitution that creates a series of equivalent objects to fill a primordial lack.

The mechanics of desire also have an economical dimension explored most fully in *Tess.* 'Now this notion of desire as an absence, lack, or hole, an abyss seeking to be engulfed, stuffed to satisfaction' continues Grosz,

is not only uniquely useful in capitalist models of acquisition, propriety, and ownership (seeing the object of desire on the model of the consumable commodity), but it also inherently sexualizes desire, coding is in terms of the prevailing characteristics attributed to the masculine/ feminine opposition, presence and absence. Desire, like female sexuality itself is insatiable, boundless, relentless, a gaping hole that cannot be filled or can only be temporarily filled; it suffers an inherent dependence on its object(s), a fundamental incompletion without them. (E. Grosz, in L. Doan, 1994, 71)

12. Lawrence Durrell, *Sebastian*, Faber, 1983, 151.

13. Bette Gordon & Karin Kay: "Look Back/ Talk Back", in P. Gibson, 1993, 91.

14. John Kucich: "Moral Authority in the Late Novels: The Gendering of Art", in H, 224.

15. B. Rich: "Compulsory Heterosexuality and Lesbian Existence", in B. Rich, 1980.

16. Becky Rosa: "Anti-monogamy: A Radical Challenge to Compulsory Heterosexuality?", in G. Griffin, 1994, 110.

17. Christobel Mackenzie: "The Anti-Sexism Campaign Invites You to Fight Sexism, Not Sex", in A. Assiter, 1993, 140.

18. Claudia: "Fear of Pornography", in A. Assiter, 1993, 132.

19. See Colleen Lamos: "The Postmodern Lesbian Position: *On Our Backs*", in L. Doan, 1994, 96; L. Butler, 1990; Case: "Toward a Butch-Femme Aesthetic", in Lynda Hart, ed. *Making a Spectacle: Feminist Essays on Contemporary Women's Theatre*, University of Michigan Press, Ann Arbor, 1989.

20. Becky Rosa: "Anti-monogamy: A Radical Challenge to Compulsory Heterosexuality?", in G. Griffin, 1994, 107.

21. Bette Gordon & Karin Kay: "Look Back/ Talk Back", in P. Gibson, 1993, 95.

22. Kristin Brady: "Textual Hysteria: Hardy's Narrator on Women", in H, 1993, 90.

23. Janet Dixon: "Separatism", *Spare Rib*, 192, 1988, 6.

24. See Alice, Gordon, Debbie and Mary: "Separatism", in S. Hoagland,

1988, 31-40; Ti-Grace Atkinson: *Amazon Odyssey*, Links Books, New York, NY, 1974; Sally Munt, 1992.

25. M. Wittig: "One is not born a woman", in S. Hoagland, 446-7. Wittig's lesbian materialist analysis of heterosexuality (in *The Straight Mind*) ignores some of the ways in which 'compulsory heterosexuality' can be subverted in a postmodern era. (Cathy Griggers: "Lesbian Bodies in the Age of (Post)-Mechanical Reproduction", in L. Doan, 1994, 124).

26. Daniel R. Schwarz: "Beginnings and Endings in Hardy's Major Fiction", in D. Kramer, 1979, 28.

27. J. Kristeva: "Romeo and Juliet: Love-Hatred in the Couple", in *Tales of Love*, 225.

28. S. Freud: "Drives and their vicissitudes", *Papers on Metapsychology*, 1915.

29. J. Kristeva: "Narcissus: The New Insanity", in *Tales of Love*, 116.

30. J. Kristeva: "Bataille and the Sun, or the Guilty Text", in *Tales of Love*, 368.

31. Perry Meisel: "Interview with Julia Kristeva", tr. Margaret Waller, *Partisan Review*, 51, Winter 1984, 131-2.

32. John Lechte: "Art, Love and Melancholy in the Work of Julia Kristeva", in J. Fletcher, 1990, 24.

33. Camille Paglia, "Love Poetry", in A. Preminger & T. Bogan, eds. *The Princeton Encyclopedia of Poetry and Poetics*, Princeton University Press, 1993.

IV   *Far From the Madding Crowd*

1. See Robert Hollander: *Boccaccio's Two Venuses*, Columbia University Press, 1977, 4.

2. The physical side of love is crucial, however, for when a kiss does occur, as when Sue is leaving Shaston, it is 'a turning-point in Jude's career' (IV. iii).

V   *The Return of the Native*

1. On Eustacia, see David Jarrett, 1973; Robert Evans, 1968; Leonard W. Deen, 1960; J.I.M. Stewart, 101-3; Pierre d'Exideuil, 21f; David Eggenschwiler, 1971.

2. R. Rehder: "The Form of Hardy's Novels", in L. Butler, 1977, 2.

3. S. de Beauvoir, in E. Marks, 152-3; Monique Wittig: "One is not born a woman", in S. Hoagland, op.cit., 440; Adrienne Rich: "Compulsory heterosexuality", op.cit.; Carolyn G. Heilbrun: *Reinventing Womanhood*, Norton, New York, NY, 1979.

VI   *The Woodlanders*

1. *The Juniper Tree and Other Tales From Grimm*, tr. Lore Segal & Randall Jarrell, Bodley Head, 1973, 57.

2. Robert Kiely: "The Menace of Solitude: The Politics and Aesthetics of Exclusion in *The Woodlanders*", in H, 191, 199

3. Mary Jacobus: "Tree and Machine: *The Woodlanders*", in D. Kramer, 1979, 120.

VII   *Tess of the d'Urbervilles*

1. M. Higonnet: "A Woman's Story: Tess and the Problem of Voice", in M. Higonnet, 1993, 15.

2. Elisabeth Bronfen: "Pay As You Go: On the Exchange of Bodies and Signs", in H, 1993, 81.

3. 'Tess was a scandalous lady in fiction in several respects' writes Christopher Walbank, 'As a victim of rape she was the mother of an illegitimate child and tainted by both in the eyes of the Victorian public' (111).

4. D. Davidson is one of many critics to discuss Hardy's use of balladry ("The Traditional Basis of Thomas Hardy's Fiction", in A. Guerard, 1986, 17).

5. The famous phrase about 'the President of the Immortals' at the end of Tess of the d'Urbervilles refers to a hunting metaphor in Classical mythology, from Aechylus' *Prometheus Bound* (I, 169). For Jean Jacques Lecercle, up until this point, Hardy's narrator in *Tess* has remained relatively distanced, but the 'President of the Immortals' sentence is a moment of 'stylistic violence':

> *What we have is an explosion of anger, irony giving way to sarcasm and rage, an instance of verbal violence, as if the pent-up energy of a narrator who so far had kept his distance has suddenly been liberated.* (in L. Butler, 1989, 1).

6. Angela Carter sees in Tess's mother a representative of the old world of superstition and folklore, which was about to disappear:

> *he [Hardy] – perfectly consciously – described a way of life at the very moment when profound change was about to begin. Tess and her sisters are themselves whirled away from that rural life deeply rooted in the past into an urban world of ceaseless and giddily accelerating change and innovation, where everything – including, or even especially, our notions of the nature of women and men – was in the melting pot, because the very idea of what constitutes 'human nature' was in the melting pot.* (A. Carter, xxi)

7. J.J. Lecercle writes: 'Tess is the sacrificed witch; she tears the veil of the civilized morality of modern society and provokes a regression to the original, founding violence' ("The Violence of Style in *Tess of the d'Urbervilles*", in L. Butler, 1989, 15).

8. L. Irigaray: *Ce sexe qui n'en est pas un*, in E. Marks, 1981, 107.

9. Jane Marcus writes that Tess is 'the great Unwed Mother', the unmarried mother as social outsider. Marcus reckons that when Tess murders Alec women 'weep for joy'. Similarly, when an abused woman hurts or kills her abuser, or is cleared of murdering her abuser in court, women cheer. 'For Tess revenges all the women wronged by men, raped, taken advantage of, impregnated, battered, harassed and despised for her lost virtue' (1981, 3).

10. Elisabeth Bronfen: "Pay As You Go: On the Exchange of Bodies and Signs", in H, 1993, 81.

11. E. Wright, 1989, 119; J. Kristeva, 1982, 237f.

12. Andrea Dworkin sees women as having one choice – 'lie or die' – not a conspiracy but a forced pretence, because '[w]omen are still basically viewed as sexual chattel – socially, legally, culturally, and in practice' (1988, 229).

13. Franz Stanzel: "Thomas Hardy: *Tess of the d'Urbervilles*", in *Der Moderne Englische Roman*, Berlin, 1963, 38f.

14. See S. Gatrell, 133; Hardy: "Candour in English Fiction", Per, 16-19. Hardy was censored (though he knew he would be in serial magazine publications); he felt he couldn't say things the way he would have liked to. Sue never says 'fuck life', though it seems she wants to say it, at times, like the old woman in Samuel Beckett's *Rockaby* who says 'fuck life' at the end of the play.

15. M. Duras, interview, *Signs*, Winter 1975, in E. Marks, 175.

16. D.H. Lawrence, *Study of Thomas Hardy*, in 1971, 222f.

17. For John Goode, in "Women and the literary text", the reader observes and is implicated in 'the objectification of Tess by the narrator which is acted out in the novel' (J. Goode, 1976, 253).

VIII   *Jude the Obscure*

1. In "Pornography and Male Supremacy", Andrea Dworkin writes that '[k]idnapping, or rape, is also the first known form of marriage – called "marriage by capture"' (1988, 229).

2. See Daniel Schwarz: "Beginnings and Endings in Hardy's Major Fiction", in D. Kramer, 1979, 33f; P. Casagrande, 1982, 203; D. Sonstroem, 1981, 9; A. Friedman, 1966, 71f.

3. Terry Eagleton sees *Jude the Obscure* as a 'calculated assault' on the reader, a deliberate flouting of the laws of realism. (T. Eagleton: "Introduction", *Jude the Obscure*, Macmillan, London, 1974).

4. 'It is true to say of him that, at his greatest, he gives us impressions; at his weakest, arguments... In *Jude the Obscure* argument is allowed to dominate impression, with the result that though the misery of the book is overwhelming, it is not tragic' (V. Woolf, *The Common Reader*, in R. Draper, 1975, 76-77).

5. For example, Susan Brownmiller: *Against Our Will: Men, Women and Rape*, Bantam, New York, NY, 1976; Barbara Toner: *The Facts of Rape*, Arrow, 1977; K. Millett, 1970; Christine Delphy: *The Main Enemy: A Materialist Analysis of Women's Oppression*, Women's Research and Resources Centre, 1977; E. Wilson: *Women and the Welfare State*, Tavistock, 1977; Susan Griffin: *Pornography and Silence: Culture's Revenge Against Nature*, Women's Press, 1981; Shulamith Firestone: *The Dialectic of Sex*, Women's Press, 1979.

6. T. Hardy, quoted in F. Pinion, 1992, 245.

7. Edmund Gosse, review in *St James's Gazette*, November 1895.

8. T. Hardy, 20 November 1895, in the Norton *Jude*, 349-350.

9. Avedon Carol & Nettie Pollard: "Changing Perception in the Feminist Debate", in A. Assiter, 1993, 52.

10. Rosemary Sumner suggests that Hardy was not quite ready to depict struggles of sexuality as well as spirit or psychology. 'This, perhaps, is the novel which would have followed *Jude* if he had written another; this, perhaps, is why it was never written' (1981, 165). But Hardy had been depicting sexual torment from his first outings into fiction, and, by *The Woodlanders*, could state, in the preface, that his intention was to explore sexual relations between men and women (39).

11. In the *Harper's* serial, this speech was extended: '"I don't see why society shouldn't be reorganized on a basis of Matriarchy – the woman and the children being the unit without the man, and the men to support the women and children collectively – not individually, as we do now."' (*Harper's*, European edition, 30, 125).

Hardy was sympathetic to the suffragette movement. 'I have for a long time been in favour of women-suffrage' he wrote in an unpublished letter to the Fawcett Society, written in 1906. He went on to discus his women-centred notions, which Phillotson proposed in *Jude the Obscure*:

I am in favour of it because I think the tendency of the women's vote will be to break up the present pernicious conventions in respect of women, customs, religion, illegitimacy, the stereotyped household (that it must be the unit of society), the father of a woman's child (that it is anybody's business but the woman's own)... (in R. Sumner, 1981, 190)

160

BIBLIOGRAPHY

All books are published in London, England, unless otherwise stated.

THOMAS HARDY

Jude the Obscure, ed. Patricia Ingham, Oxford University Press, 1985
Jude the Obscure: An Authoritative Text, Backgrounds and Sources, Criticism, ed. Norman Page, W.W. Norton & Co, New York, NY, 1978
Tess of the D'Urbervilles, ed. David Skilton, Penguin, 1978/85
Tess of the D'Urbervilles: An Authoritative Text, Hardy and the Novel, ed. Scott Elledge, W.W. Norton & Co, New York, NY, 1965/79
Tess of the d'Urbervilles, eds. Juliet Grindle & Simon Gatrell, Oxford University Press, 1983
Tess of the d'Urbervilles, World Classics, eds. Juliet Grindle & Simon Gatrell, Oxford University Press, 1988
"*Tess of the d'Urbervilles*", *Graphic*, XLIV, July-December, 1891
The Return of the Native, ed. George Woodcock, Penguin, 1978
The Woodlanders, ed. James Gibson, Penguin, 1981
The Mayor of Casterbridge, ed. Martin Seymour-Smith, Penguin, 1985
Under the Greenwood Tree, ed. Simon Gatrell, Oxford University Press, 1985
A Pair of Blue Eyes, ed. Alan Manford, Oxford University Press, 1985
The Well-Beloved, ed. Tom Hetherington, Oxford University Press, 1986
Two on a Tower, ed. F.B. Pinion, Macmillan, London, 1975
A Laocidean, Heron/ Macmillan, London, 1987
The Hand of Ethelberta, ed. Robert Gittings, Macmillan, London, 1975
The Trumpet-Major, St Martins Library, Macmillan, London, 1962
Complete Poems, ed. James Gibson, Macmillan, London, 1981
Selected Poems, ed. Walford Davies, Dent, 1982

Selected Short Poems, ed. John Wain, Macmillan, London, 1966/75

The Gates Along the Path: Poems, Terra Nova Editions, 1979

Hardy's Love Poems, ed. Carl J. Weber, Macmillan, London, 1983

The Short Stories of Thomas Hardy, Macmillan, London, 1928

The Literary Notebooks of Thomas Hardy, ed. Lennart A. Björk, 2 vols, Macmillan, 1985

The Collected Letters of Thomas Hardy, eds. Richard Little Purdy & Michael Millgate, 7 vols, Clarendon Press, 1978-88

Thomas Hardy's Notebooks, ed. Evelyn Hardy, Hogarth Press, 1955

The Personal Notebooks of Thomas Hardy, ed. Richard H. Taylor, Macmillan, London, 1978

The Life of Thomas Hardy, Macmillan, London, 1962

The Life and Work of Thomas Hardy, ed. Michael Millgate, Macmillan, London, 1984

Personal Writings, ed. Harold Orel, Macmillan, London, 1967

Thomas Hardy's "Studies, Specimens &c" Notebook, eds. P. Dalziel & M. Millgate, Clarendon Press, Oxford, 1994

Thomas Hardy's Public Voice, ed. M. Millgate, Clarendon Press, Oxford, 2001

OTHERS

Gary Adelman. *Jude the Obscure: A Paradise of Despair*, Twayne, New York, NY, 1992

John Alcorn. *The Nature Novel from Hardy to Lawrence*, Macmillan, London, 1973

Patricia Alden. *Social Mobility in the English Bildungsroman*, UMI Research Press, Ann Arbor, 1986

A. Alexander. *Thomas Hardy: The "Dream-Country" of His Fiction*, London: Vision, 1987.

B.J. Alexander. "Anti-Christian Elements in Thomas Hardy's Novels", *DAI*, 36, 1975

Wayne Anderson. "The Rhetoric of Silence in Hardy's Fiction", *Studies in the Novel*, 17, 1985

T. Armstrong. *Haunted Hardy*, Palgrave Macmillan, London, 2000

Alison Assister & Avedon Carol, eds. *Bad Girls and Dirty Pictures: The Challenge to Reclaim Feminism*, Pluto Press, 1993

D.F. Barber, ed. *Concerning Thomas Hardy*, Charles Skilton, 1968

J.O. Bailey. *The Poetry of Thomas Hardy*, University of North Carolina

Press, Chapel Hill 1970

A. Banerjee, ed. *An Historical Evaluation of Thomas Hardy's Poetry,* Edwin Mellen Press, 2001

N. Barber & P. Lee-Browne. *Thomas Hardy,* Evans Brothers, 2000

Regina Barreca, ed. *Sex and Death in Victorian Literature,* Indiana University Press, Bloomington, 1990

John Barrell. "Geographies of Hardy's Wessex", *Journal of Historical Geography,* 8, 1982

John Bayley. *An Essay on Hardy,* Cambridge University Press, 1978

R. Bell & R. Klein, eds. *Radically Speaking: Feminism Reclaimed,* Spinifex, North Melbourne, 1996

S. Berger. *Thomas Hardy and Visual Structures: Framing, Disruption, Process,* New York University Press, New York, NY, 1990.

Philippa Berry & Andrew Wernick, eds. *Shadow of Spirit: Postmodernism and Religion,* Routledge, 1992

Kathleen Blake. "Pure Tess: Thomas Hardy on Knowing a Woman", *Studies in English Literature,* 22, 1982

Paula Blank. *"Tess of the d'Urbervilles":* The English Novel and the Foreign Plot", *Mid-Hudson Language Studies,* 12, 1989

Harold Bloom, ed. *Thomas Hardy: Modern Critical Views,* Chelsea House, New York, NY, 1987

—. ed. *Thomas Hardy's Tess of the d'Urbervilles,* Chelsea House Publishers, New York, NY, 1996

—. *Thomas Hardy,* Chelsea House Publishers, New York, NY, 2003

E. Blunden. *Thomas Hardy,* London, 1942

R. Blythe. *Characters and Their Landscapes,* Harcout Brace Jovanovitch, New York, NY, 1983

Charlotte Bonica. "Nature and Paganism in Hardy's *Tess",* *Journal of English Literary History,* 49, 4 1982

F. Bonner *et al*, eds. *Imagining Women Cultural Representations and Gender,* Polity Press, Cambridge, 1992

Penny Boumelha. *Thomas Hardy and Women: Sexual Ideology and Narrative,* Harvester, 1982

A. Brick. "Paradise and Consciousness in Hardy's *Tess",* *19th Century Fiction,* 17, 1962

J. Bristow & A. Wilson, eds. *Activating Theory, Gay, Bisexual Politics,* Lawrence & Wishart, London, 1993

—. *Effeminate England: Homosexuality After 1885,* Open University Press, Milton Keynes, 1995

Jean Brooks. *Thomas Hardy: The Poetic Structure,* Elek, 1971

B. Brown & P. Adams: "The feminine body and feminist politics", *M/F,* 3, 1979

Douglas Brown. *Thomas Hardy,* Longmans, Green & Co., 1954

—. *Thomas Hardy: 'The Mayor of Casterbridge',* Arnold, 1962

S.H. Brown. ""Tess" and Tess: An Experiment in Genre", *Modern Fiction*

Studies, 28, 1, 1982

J.H. Buckley. "Tess and the d'Urbervilles", *Victorian Institute Journal*, 20, 1992

J.B. Bullen. *The Expressive Eye: Fiction of Perception in the Work of Thomas Hardy*, Clarendon Press, 1986

Peter J. Burgard, ed. *Nietzsche and the Feminine*, University Press, of Virginia, Charlottesville, 1994

L. Bushloper. "Hardy's *Tess of the D'Urbervilles*," *Explicator*, 52:4, 1994

Judith Butler. *Gender Trouble: Feminism and the Subversion of Identity*, Routledge, 1990

Lance St. John Butler, ed. *Thomas Hardy, After Fifty Years*, Macmillan, London, 1977

—. ed. *Alternative Hardy*, Macmillan, London, 1989

—. *Thomas Hardy*, Cambridge University Press, 1978

Elizabeth Campbell. "*Tess of the d'Urbervilles*: Misfortune Is a Woman", *Victorian Newsletter*, 70, 1989

Glen Cavaliero. *The Rural Tradition in the English Novel 1900-1939*, Macmillan, London, 1977

Joseph Campbell. *The Power of Myth*, with Bill Moyers, ed. Betty Sue Flowers, Doubleday, New York, NY, 1988

Richard Carpenter. *Thomas Hardy*, Macmillan, London, 1978

Norman T. Carrington. *The Mayor of Casterbridge*, Pan, 1976

Peter J. Casagrande. *Hardy's Influence on the Modern Novel*, Palgrave Macmillan, London, 1987

—. *Unity in Thomas Hardy's Novels*, Regents, Lawrence, 1982

—. *Tess of the d'Urbervilles: Unorthodox Beauty*, Twayne, New York, NY, 1992

David Cecil. *Hardy the Novelist*, Constable, 1943

J. Chandler, ed. *Thomas Hardy's Christmas*, Sutton Publishing, 1997

S. Chandra. *Thomas Hardy*, Sangam Books, 1999

R. Chapman. *The Language of Thomas Hardy*, Macmillan, London, 1990

Mary E. Chase. *Thomas Hardy From Serial to Novel*, University of Minnesota Press, 1927

Gail Chester & Julienne Dickey, ed. *Feminism and Censorship: The Current Debate*, Prism Press, Bridport, Dorset, 1988

Mary Childers. "Thomas Hardy, the Man Who 'Liked' Women", *Criticism*, 23, 1981

Hélène Cixous. *The Hélène Cixous Reader*, ed. Susan Sellers, Blackwell, 1994

—. *The Newly Born Woman*, tr. Betsy Wing, Minnesota University Press, Minneapolis, 1986

Laura Claridge. "Tess: A Less Than Pure Woman Ambivalently Presented", *Texas Studies in Literature and Language*, 28, 3, 1986

—. & Elizabeth Langland, eds. *Out of Bounds: Male Writers and Gender(ed) Criticism*, University Massachusetts Press, Amherst, 1990

G. Clarke, ed. *Thomas Hardy: Critical Assessments*, Helm Information, 1993

P. Clements & J. Grindle, eds. *The Poetry of Thomas Hardy*, London, 1980

D. Collins. *Thomas Hardy and His God: A Liturgy of Unbelief*, Macmillan, London, 1990

Vere H. Collins. *Talks With Thomas Hardy at Max Gate*, Duckworth, 1972

Alex Comfort. *I and That*, Beazley, 1979

W.V. Costanzo. "Polanski in Wessex: Filming *Tess of the d'Urbervilles*", *Literature/ Film Quarterly*, 9, 2, 1981

J. Stevens Cox, ed. *Thomas Hardy Yearbook*, Toucan Press, various dates

R.G. Cox, ed. *Thomas Hardy: The Critical Heritage*, Barnes & Noble 1970

R. Craik. "Hardy's *Tess of the D'Urbervilles*", *Explicator*, 53:1, 1994

Louis Crompton. "The Sunburnt God: Ritual and Tragic Myth in *The Return of the Native*", *Boston University Studies in English*, 4, 1960

Gail Cunningham. *The New Woman and the Victorian Novel*, Macmillan, London, 1978

H.M. Daleski. "*Tess*: Mastery and Abandon", *Essays in Criticism*, 30, 1980

—. *Thomas Hardy and Paradoxes of Love*, University of Missouri Press, Columbia, MO, 1997

Jagdish Chandra Dave. *The Human Predicament in Hardy's Novels*, Macmillan, London, 1985

Donald Davie. *Thomas Hardy and British Poetry*, Routledge & Kegan Paul, 1979

—. *With the Grain: Essays on Thomas Hardy and Modern British Poetry*, Carcanet Press, Manchester, 1998

W. Davis, Jr. "The Rape of Tess: Hardy, English Law, and the Case for Sexual Assault", *Nineteenth Century Literature*, 52:2, 1997

Lois Deacon & Terry Coleman. *Providence and Mr. Hardy*, Hutchinson, 1966

D. De Laura. "The Ache of Modernism in Hardy's Later Novels", Sept, 1967

B. DeMille. "Cruel Illusions: Nietzsche, Conrad, Hardy, and the 'Shadowy Ideal'", *SEL*, 30:4, 1990

Laura Doan, ed. *The Lesbian Postmodern*, Columbia University Press, New York, NY, 1994

Mary Ann Doane. *The Desire to Desire: The Woman's Film of the 1940's*, Macmillan, London, 1987

Margaret Drabble, ed. *The Genius of Thomas Hardy*, Weidenfeld & Nicolson, 1976

J. Drake. *Thomas Hardy*, Wessex Books, 1999

—. ed. *A Writer's Britain*, Thames & Hudson, 1979

R.P. Draper, ed. *Thomas Hardy: Three Pastoral Novels*, Macmillan, London, 1987

—. ed. *Hardy: The Tragic Novels*, Macmillan, London, 1975

H.C. Duffin. *Thomas Hardy*, Greenwood Press, Conn., 1978

S. Dutta. *Ambivalence in Hardy*, Palgrave Macmillan, London, 1999

Andrea Dworkin. *Intercourse*, Arrow, 1988

—. *Pornography: Men Possessing Women*, Women's Press, 1984

Mary Eagleton, ed. *Feminist Literary Criticism*, Longman, 1991

Terry Eagleton. "Thomas Hardy: Nature as Language", *Critical Quarterly*, Summer, 1971

—. *The Eagleton Reader*, Blackwell, Oxford, 1998

Roger Ebbatson. *Lawrence and the Nature Tradition*, Harvester Press, Brighton 1980

—. "The Plutonic Master: Hardy and the Steam Threshing Machine", *Critical Survey*, 2, 1990

—. *Hardy: The Margin of the Unexpressed*, Sheffield Academic Press, 1994

S. Eddy. *Thomas Hardy (Pre-1914 Classics Series)*, Folens Publishers, 2000

Anne-Marie Edwards. *Discovering Hardy's Wessex*, BBC, 1978

D. Eggenschwiler. "Eustacia Vye, Queen of the Night and Courtly Pretender", *Nineteenth Century Fiction*, 25, 1971

H. Eilberg-Schwartz & W. Doniger, eds. *Off With Her Head! The Denial of Women's Identity in Myth, Religion, and Culture*, University of California Press, Berkeley, 1995

Ralph W.V. Elliott. *Thomas Hardy's English*, Basil Blackwell, 1984

D. Ellis & H. Mills. *D.H. Lawrence's Non-Fiction: Art, Thought and Genre*, Cambridge University Press, Cambridge, 1988

—. *D.H. Lawrence: The Dying Game, 1922-30*, Cambridge University Press, Cambridge, 1998

A. Enstice. *Thomas Hardy*, London, 1979

R. Evans. "The Other Eustacia", *Novel*, 1, 1968

M. Farwell. *Heterosexual Plots and Lesbian Narratives*, New York University Press, 1996

A. Fischler. "An Affinity for Birds: Kindness in Hardy's *Jude the Obscure*", *Studies in the Novel*, 13:3, 1981

—. "Gins and Spirits: The Letter's Edge in Hardy's *Jude the Obscure*", *Studies in the Novel*, 16:1, 1984

Joe Fisher. *The Hidden Hardy*, Macmillan, London, 1992

Alexander Fischler. "Gins and Spirits: The Letter's Edge in Hardy's *Jude the Obscure*", *SNNTS*, 16, 1984

John Fletcher & Andrew Benjamin, ed. *Abjection, Melancholia and Love: the Work of Julia Kristeva*, Routledge, 1990

John Fowles & Jo Draper. *Thomas Hardy's England*, Cape, 1984

Janet Freeman. "Ways of Looking at Tess", *Studies in Philology*, 79, 3, 1982

Alan Friedman. *The Turn of the Novel*, Oxford University Press, 1966

—. ed. *Forms of Modern Fiction*, Austin, 1975

Lorraine Gamman & Margaret Marshment, eds. *The Female Gaze: Women as Viewers of Popular Culture*, Women's Press 1988

M. Garber. *Vested Interests: Cross-Dressing and Cultural Anxiety*, Routledge, London, 1992

—. *Vice Versa: Bisexuality and the Eroticism of Everyday Life*, Simon & Schuster, NY, 1995

Marjorie Garson. *Hardy's Fables of Integrity: Woman, Body, Text*, Oxford University Press, 1991

Simon Gatrell, ed. *The Thomas Hardy Archive 1: Tess of the d'Urbervilles*, Garland, New York, NY, 1986

—. *Hardy the Creator: A Textual Biography*, Clarendon Press, 1988

—. *Thomas Hardy and the Proper Study of Mankind*, Macmillan, London, 1993

E. Gemmette. "George Eliot's *Mill on the Floss* and Hardy's *Jude the Obscure*", *Explicator*, 42:3, 1984

Helmut E. Gerber & W. Eugene Davis, eds. *Thomas Hardy: An Annotated Bibliography of Writings About Him*, Northern Illinois University Press, 1973

James Gibson, ed. *Thomas Hardy and History*, Palgrave Macmillan, London, 1974

—. & Trevor Johnson, eds. *Thomas Hardy: Poems: A Casebook*, Macmillan, 1979

—. Thomas Hardy, Palgrave Macmillan, London, 1996

Pamela Church Gibson & Roma Gibson, eds. *Dirty Looks: Women, Pornography, Power*, British Film Institute, 1993

R. Giddings & E. Sheen, eds. *The Classic Novel From Page to Screen*, Manchester University Press, 2000

Robert Gittings. *Young Thomas Hardy*, London, 1975

—. *The Older Hardy*, Heinemann, 1978

—. & J. Manton: *The Second Mrs Hardy*, London, 1979

John Goode. "Sue Bridehead and the New Woman", in M. Jacobus, 1979

—. *Thomas Hardy: The Offensive Truth*, Basil Blackwell, 1988

W. Goetz. "Felicity and Infelicity of Marriage in *Tess of the d'Urbervilles*", *Nineteenth Century Fiction*, 38, 1983

William Greenslade. *Degeneration, Culture and the Novel 1880-1940*, Cambridge, 1994

Ian Gregor. *The Great Web*, Faber, 1974

J. Gribble. "The Quiet Women of Egdon Heath", *Essays In Criticism*, 46, 1996

Gabriele Griffin *et al*, eds. *Stirring It: Challenges For Feminism*, Taylor & Francis, 1994

E. Grosz. "Philosophy, Subjectivity and the Body", in C. Pateman & E. Grosz, eds., *Feminist Challenges*, Allen & Unwin, Sydney, 1986

—. "Desire, the body and recent French feminism", *Intervention*, 21-2, 1988

—. *Sexual Subversions*, Allen & Unwin, London, 1989

—. "The Body of Signification", in J. Fletcher, 1990

167

—. *Jacques Lacan: A Feminist Introduction*, Routledge, London, 1990

—. "Lesbian fetishism?", *Differences*, 3, 2, 1991

—. "Fetishization", in E. Wright, 1992

—. "Julia Kristeva", in E. Wright, 1992

—. *Voltaile Bodies*, Indiana University Press, Bloomington, 1994

—. "Refiguring Lesbian Desire", in L. Doan, 1994

—. *Space, Time and Perversion*, Routledge, London, 1995

Peter Grundy. "Linguistics and Literary Criticism: A Marriage of Convenience", *English*, 30, 137, 1981

Albert J. Guerard. *Thomas Hardy*, Oxford University Press, 1949

—. ed. *Hardy: A Collection of Critical Essays*, Prentice-Hall International, New York, NY, 1963/86

F.E. Halliday. *Thomas Hardy*, Adams & Dart, Bath, 1972

G. Handley. *Thomas Hardy: Tess of the d'Urbervilles*, Penguin Critical Studies, Penguin, 1991

T. Hands, T. *Thomas Hardy: Distracted Preacher?*, London, 1989

—. *A Hardy Chronology* London, 1992

—. *Thomas Hardy*, Macmillan, London, 1995

B. Hardy. *Thomas Hardy*, Athlone, London, 2000

Evelyn Hardy. *The Countryman's Ear*, Tebb House, Padstow, Cornwall, 1982

Margaret Harris. "Thomas Hardy's *Tess of the d'Urbervilles*: Faithfully presented by Roman Polanski", *Sydney Studies in English*, 7, 1982

L. Hart. *Between the Body and the Flesh: Performing Sadomasochism*, Columbia University Press, 1998

G. Harvey. *The Complete Critical Guide to Thomas Hardy*, Routledge, London, 2003

M.E. Hassett. "Compromised Romanticism in *Jude the Obscure*", *Nineteenth Century Fiction*, 25, 1971

Desmond Hawkins. *Hardy's Wessex*, Macmillan, London, 1983

—. *Hardy: Novelist and Poet*, David & Charles, Devon, 1976

Jeremy Hawthorn, ed. *The Nineteenth-Century British Novel*, Arnold 1986

Stephen Hazell, ed. *The English Novel*, Macmillan, London, 1978

J. Hazen. "The Tragedy of Tess Durbeyfield", *Texas Studies in Literature and Language*, 11, 1969

R. Heilman. "Hardy's Sue Bridehead", *Nineteenth Century Fiction*, 20, 1966

Susan J. Hekman. *Gender and Knowledge: Elements of a Postmodern Feminism*, Polity Press, 1990

Lucille Herbert. "Hardy's Views in Tess of the d'Urbervilles", *English Literary History*, 37, 1970

Margaret R. Higonnet, ed. "Fictions of Feminine Voice: Antiphony and Silence in Hardy's *Tess of the d'Urbervilles*", in L. Claridge, 1990

—. *The Sense of Sex: Feminist Perspectives on Hardy*, University of Illinois Press, Urbana, 1993

168

G.G. Hiller, ed. *Poems of the Elizabethan Age*, Methuen, 1977

Sarah Lucia Hoagland & Julia Penelope, eds. *For Lesbians Only: A separatist anthology*, Onlywomen Press, 1988

Bert G. Hornback. *The Metaphor of Chance: Vision and Technique in the Works of Thomas Hardy*, Ohio University Press, Athens, 1971

L. Horne. "Symbol and Structure in *Jude the Obscure*", *Literatur in Wissenschaft und Unterricht*, 11, 1978

Irving Howe. *Thomas Hardy*, Macmillan, London, 1985

Maggie Humm. *Feminisms: A Reader*, Harvester Wheatsheaf, 1992

—. *Practising Feminist Criticism*, Prentice-Hall 1995

—. ed. *A Reader's Guide to Contemporary Feminist Literary Criticism*, Prentice-Hall 1995

—. ed. *The Dictionary of Feminist Theory*, Harvester Wheatsheaf, 1989/ 1995

Virginia R. Hyman. *Ethical Perspectives in the Novels of Thomas Hardy*, Kenniket Press, New York, NY, 1975

S. Hynes. *The Pattern of Hardy's Poetry*, London, 1961

Patricia Ingham. *Thomas Hardy*, Harvester Wheatsheaf, Hemel Hempstead 1989

Luce Irigaray. *This Sex Which Is Not One*, tr. C. Porter & C. Burke, Cornell University Press, New York, NY, 1977

—. *Speculum of the Other Woman*, tr. G.C. Gill, Cornell University Press, New York, NY, 1985

—. *The Irigaray Reader*, ed. Margaret Whitford, Blackwell, Oxford, 1991

—. *Je, tu, nous: Toward a Culture of Difference*, tr. Alison Martin, Routledge, 1993

—. *Thinking the Difference: For a Peaceful Revolution*, Athlone Press, 1994

M. Irwin. *Reading Hardy's Landscapes*, Palgrave Macmillan, London, 2000

Arlene M. Jackson. *Illustration and the Novels of Thomas Hardy*, Macmillan, London, 1981

S. Jackson & J. Jones, eds. *Contemporary Feminist Theories*, Edinburgh University Press, 1998

Mary Jacobus. "Sue the Obscure", *Essays in Criticism*, 25, 1975

—. "Tess's Purity", *Essays in Criticism*, 26, 1976

—. ed. *Women Writing and Writing About Women*, Croom Helm, 1979

—. "Tess: The Making of a Pure Woman", in Bloom, 1987

—. "Hardy's Magian Retrospective", *Essays in Criticism*, 32, 1982

—. *Reading Woman: essays in feminist criticism*, Methuen, 1986

G.M. Jantzen. *Becoming Divine: Towards a Feminist Philosophy of Religion*, Manchester University Press, 1998

J. Jedrzejewski. *Thomas Hardy and the Church*, Palgrave Macmillan, London, 1995

Trevor Johnson. *Thomas Hardy*, Evans Brothers, 1968

Ann Rosalind Jones. "Writing the Body: Toward an Understanding of

L'Écriture féminine", in E. Showalter, 1986

J. Juffer. *At Home With Pornography: Women, Sex and Everyday Life,* New York University Press, 1998

Denis Kay-Robinson. *The Landscape of Thomas Hardy,* Webb & Bower, 1987

—. *Hardy's Wessex Reappraised,* David & Charles, Newton Abbot, Devon 1972

—. *The First Mrs Thomas Hardy,* London, 1979

W.J. Keith. *Regions of the Imagination: The Development of the British Rural Tradition,* University of Toronto Press, Toronto, 1988

—. *The Poetry of Nature: Rural Perspectives in Poetry From Wordsworth to the Present,* University of Toronto Press, Toronto, 1980

A. Kettle. *Hardy the Novelist,* University of Wales Press, Swansea, 1967

James Kincaid: "Hardy's Absences", in D. Kramer, 1979

M. Kinkead-Weekes, ed. *Twentieth-Century Interpretations of The Rainbow,* Prentice-Hall, New Jersey, 1971

—. *D.H. Lawrence: Triumph to Exile, 1912-1922,* Cambridge University Press, Cambridge, 1996

Dale Kramer. *Thomas Hardy: The Forms of Tragedy,* Macmillan, London, 1975

—. ed. *Critical Approaches to the Fiction of Thomas Hardy,* Barnes, Totowa, 1979

—. ed. *Critical Essays on Thomas Hardy: The Novels,* G.K Hall, 1990

—. *Tess of the d'Urbervilles,* Cambridge University Press, 1991

—. ed. *The Cambridge Companion to Thomas Hardy,* Cambridge University Press, Cambridge, 1999

Julia Kristeva. *Desire in Language: A Semiotic Approach to Literature and Art,* ed. Leon Roudiez, tr. Thomas Gora, Alice Jardine & Leon Roudiez, Blackwell, 1982

—. *The Kristeva Reader,* ed. Toril Moi, Blackwell, 1986

—. *Tales of Love,* tr. Leon S. Roudiez, Columbia University Press, New York, NY, 1987

—. *About Chinese Women,* tr. A. Barrows, Boyars, 1977

—. *Powers of Horror: An Essay on Abjection,* tr. Leon S. Roudiez, Columbia University Press, New York, NY, 1982

—. *Revolution in Poetic Language,* tr. Margaret Walker, Columbia University Press, New York, NY, 1984

—. "A Question of Subjectivity: an interview" [with Susan Sellers], *Women's Review,* 12, 1986, in P. Rice, 1992

Weston La Barre. *The Ghost Dance,* Allen & Unwin, 1972

—. *Muelos,* Columbia University Press, New York, NY, 1985

Jacques Lacan and the *École Freudienne: Feminine Sexuality,* ed. Juliet Mitchell and Jacqueline Rose, Macmillan, London, 1982

—. *Écrits: A Selection,* tr. Alan Sheridan, Tavistock, 1977

J.T. Laird. *The Shaping of "Tess of the d'Urbervilles",* Oxford University

Press, 1975

—. "New Light on the Evolution of *Tess of the d'Urbervilles*", *Review of English Studies*, 31, 124, 1980

C. Lane. *The Burdens of Intimacy: Psychoanalysis and Victorian Masculinity*, Chicago University Press, 1999

R. Langbaum. *Thomas Hardy in Our Time*, Palgrave Macmillan, London, 1997

Elizabeth Langland. "A Perspective of One's Own: Thomas Hardy and the Elusive Sue Bridehead", *Studies in the Novel*, 12, 1980

—. *Gothic Manners and the Classic English Novel*, University of Wisconsin Press, Madison, 1988

—. "Masculinity in *Jude the Obscure*", in M. Higonnet, 1993

Albert J. LaValley, ed. *Tess of the D'Urbervilles: A Collection of Critical Essays*, Prentice-Hall, New Jersey, 1969

D.H. Lawrence. *Study of Thomas Hardy and Other Essays*, ed. Bruce Steele, Cambridge University Press, 1985

—. *A Selection from Phoenix*, ed. A.A.H. Inglis, Penguin, 1971

—. *Selected Essays*, Penguin, 1950

—. *The Rainbow*, ed. John Worthen, Penguin, 1981/6

—. *The Complete Short Novels*, ed. Keith Sagar & Melissa Partridge, Penguin, 1982/7

—. *Aaron's Rod*, Penguin, 1950

—. *Sons and Lovers*, ed. Keith Sagar, Penguin, 1981/6

—. *Kangaroo*, Penguin, 1950

Herman Lea. *Thomas Hardy's Wessex*, Macmillan, London, 1977

Glenda Leeming. *Who's Who in Thomas Hardy*, Elm Tree, 1975

Lawrence Lerner & John Holmstrom. *Thomas Hardy and His Readers*, Bodley Head, 1968

J. LeVay. "Hardy's *Jude the Obscure*", *Explicator*, 49:4, 1991

Charles Lock. *Thomas Hardy: Criticism in Focus*, Bristol Classic Press, 1992

David Lodge. *Language of Fiction*, Routledge & Kegan Paul, 1966

Bryan Longhrey, ed. *Critical Survey*, Thomas Hardy number, 5, 2, 1983

Jakob Lothe. "Hardy's Authorial Narrative Methods in *Tess of the d'Urbervilles*", in J. Hawthorn, 1986

John Lucas. *The Literature of Change*, Harvester, 1977

Phillip V. Mallett & Ronald P. Draper, eds. *A Spacious Vision: Essays on Hardy*, Patten Press, Penzance, 1994

—. "Sexual Ideology and Narrative Form in *Jude the Obscure*", *English*, 38:162, 1989

—. ed. *Thomas Hardy: Texts and Contexts*, Palgrave Macmillan, London, 2002

Jane Marcus. "A Tess For Child Molesters", *Jump Cut*, 3, 1981

Elaine Marks & Isabelle de Courtivron, eds. *New French Feminisms: an anthology*, Harvester Wheatsheaf, 1981

K. Marsden. *The Poems of Thomas Hardy: A Critical Introduction*, London, 1969

Karl Marx, *Selected Works*, I, Lawrence & Wishart, 1942

K. Maynard. *Thomas Hardy's Tragic Poetry*, University of Iowa Press, 1991

L. McQuiston. *Suffragettes to She-Devils: Women's Liberation and Beyond*, Phaidon, London, 1997

R. McRuer. *The Queer Renaissance*, New York University Press, New York, NY, 1997

Helena Michie. *The Flesh Made Word: Female Figures and Women's Bodies*, Oxford University Press, 1987

Ruth Milberg-Kaye. *Thomas Hardy: Myths of Sexuality*, John Jay Press, New York, NY, 1983

R. Miles. "The Women of Wessex", in A. Smith, 1979

J. Hillis Miller. *Thomas Hardy: Distance and Desire*, Oxford University Press, 1970

—. *Fiction and Repetition: Seven English Novels*, Harvard University Press, 1982

Kate Millett. *Sexual Politics*, Doubleday, Garden City, 1970

Michael Millgate. *Thomas Hardy: His Career as a Novelist*, Bodley Head, 1971

—. *Thomas Hardy: A Biography*, Oxford University Press, 1982

W. Mitsichelli. "Androgyny, Survival, and Fulfilment in Thomas Hardy's *Far From the Madding Crowd*", *Modern Language Studies*, 18, 3, 1988

Toril Moi. *Sexual/Textual Politics: Feminist Literary Theory*, Routledge, 1988

—. ed. *French Feminist Thought*, Blackwell, 1988

Rosemarie Morgan. *Women and Sexuality in the Novels of Thomas Hardy*, Routledge, 1988

Roy Morrell. *Thomas Hardy: The Will and the Way*, University of Malaysia Press, 1965

R.D. Morrison. "Reading and Restoration in *Tess of the d'Urbervilles*", *Victorian Newsletter*, 82, 1992

Sally Munt, ed. *New Lesbian Criticism: Literary and Cultural Readings*, Harvester Wheatsheaf, 1992

Lynda Nead. *Female Nude: Art, Obscenity and Sexuality*, Routledge, 1992

E. Neill. *Trial by Ordeal: Thomas Hardy and the Critics*, Camden House, 1999

—. *The Secret Life of Thomas Hardy*, Ashgate Publishing, 2004

P. Niemeyer. *Seeing Hardy*, McFarland & Company, 2002

H. Orel. *The Final Years of Thomas Hardy 1912-1928*, London, 1976

—. *Thomas Hardy's Epic Drama: A Study of 'The Dynasts*, Kansas, 1963

Timothy O'Sullivan. *Thomas Hardy: An Illustrated Biography*, Macmillan, London, 1981

T. O'Toole. *Genealogy and Fiction in Hardy*, Palgrave Macmillan, London,

1997

Norman Page, ed. *Thomas Hardy: The Writer and His Background,* Bell & Hyman, 1980

—. ed. *Thomas Hardy Annual,* Macmillan, London, 1983-

—. & Peter Preston, eds. *The Literature of Place,* Macmillan, London, 1993

—. *Thomas Hardy: Family History,* Routledge/ Thoemmes Press, 1998

—. ed. *The Oxford Reader's Companion to Hardy,* Oxford University Press, Oxford, 2000

B. Paris. ""A Confusion of Many Standards": Conflicting Value Systems in *Tess of the d'Urbervilles",* Nineteenth Century Fiction, 24, 1970

Lynn Parker. ""Pure Woman" and Tragic Heroine? Conflicting Myths in Hardy's *Tess of the d'Urbervilles",* Studies in the Novel, 24, 1992

J. Paterson. *"The Return of the Native* as Antichristian Document", *Nineteenth Century Fiction,* 14, 1959

—. *The Making of 'The Return of the Native',* University of California Press, 1960

M. Patil. *Thomas Hardy, the Poet,* Atlantic Publishers, 1998

Michael Payne. *Reading Theory: An Introduction to Lacan, Derrida, and Kristeva,* Blackwell, 1993

John Peck. *How to Study a Thomas Hardy Novel,* Macmillan, London, 1983

Charles P.C. Petit, ed. *New Perspectives on Thomas Hardy,* Macmillan, London, 1994

—. ed. *Reading Thomas Hardy,* Palgrave Macmillan, London, 1998

F.B. Pinion. *A Hardy Companion,* Macmillan, London, 1968

—. ed. *Thomas Hardy and the Modern World,* Thomas Hardy Society, Dorchester, 1974

—. *Thomas Hardy: Art and Thought,* Macmillan, London, 1977

—. ed. *A Thomas Hardy Dictionary,* Palgrave Macmillan, 1992

Monique Plaza. ""Phallomorphic power" and the psychology of "woman"", *Ideology and Consciousness,* 4, 1978

M. Ponsford. "Thomas Hardy's Control of Sympathy in *Tess of the D'Urbervilles",* Midwest Quarterly, 27:4 1986

Adrian Poole. "Men's Words and Hardy's Women", *Essays in Criticism,* 31, 1981

C.L. Preston. *A KWIC Concordance to Thomas Hardy's Tess of the d'Urbervilles,* Garland, New York, NY, 1989

R.L. Purdy. *Thomas Hardy: A Bibliography Study,* Oxford University Press, 1954

Lyn Pykett. "Ruinous bodies: women and sexuality in Hardy's late fiction", in B. Longhrey, 1983

John Rabbets. *From Hardy to Faulkner: Wessex to Yoknapatawpha,* Macmillan, London, 1989

A. Radford. *Thomas Hardy and the Survivals of Time,* Ashgate Publishing, 2003

H. Radner. *Shopping Around: Feminine Culture and the Pursuit of Pleasure,*

Routledge, New York, NY, 1995

P. Ralph. *Hardy's Geography*, Palgrave Macmillan, London, 2002

M. Ray. *An Annotated Critical Bibliography of Thomas Hardy*, London, 1989

—. *Thomas Hardy*, Ashgate, Aldershot, 1997

Philip Rice & Patricia Waugh, eds. *Modern Literary Theory: A Reader*, Arnold 1992

Adrienne Rich. *Blood, Bread and Poetry*, Virago, 1980

—. *Of Woman Born: Motherhood as Experience and Institution*, Virago, 1977

Jeanne Addison Roberts. *The Shakespearean Wild: Geography, Genus and Gender*, University of Nebraska Press, Lincoln, Nebraska 1991

Katherine Rogers. "Women in Thomas Hardy", *Centennial Review*, 19, 1975

R. Saldivar. "*Jude the Obscure*: Reading and the Spirit of the Law", *English Literary History*, 50:3, 1983

C.H. Salter. *Good Little Thomas Hardy*, Macmillan, London, 1981

B. Santangelo. "A Moral Dilemma: Ethics in *Tess of the D'Urbervilles*", *English Studies*, 75:1, 1994

J. Schad. *Victorians in Theory From Derrida to Browning*, Manchester University Press, 1999

Nadine Schoenburg. "The Supernatural in *Tess*", *Thomas Hardy Yearbook*, 19, 1989

Arthur Schopenhauer. *Essays and Aphorisms*, Penguin, 1970

J. Shumaker. "Breaking with the Conventions: Victorian Confession Novels and *Tess of the D'Urbervilles*", *English Literature in Transition (1880-1920)*, 37:4, 1994

Robert Schweik, "Moral Perspective in *Tess of the D'Urbervilles*", *College English* 24, 1962

—. "Theme, Character and Perspective in Hardy's *The Return of the Native*", *Philological Quarterly*, 41, 1962

Janie Sénèchal. "Focalisation, Regard et Désire dans *Far From the Madding Crowd*," *Cahiers Victoriens et Edouardiens*, 12, 1980

Martin Seymour-Smith. *Hardy*, Bloomsbury, 1994

Charles Shapiro, ed. *Twelve Original Essays on Great English Novels*, Detroit 1960

G.W. Sherman. *The Pessimism of Thomas Hardy*, Associated University Press, New Jersey, 1976

J. Sherrick. *Thomas Hardy's Major Novels*, Scarecrow Press, 1998

Elaine Showalter, ed. *The New Feminist Criticism*, Virago 1986

Kaja Silverman. "History, Figuration and Female Subjectivity in *Tess of the d'Urbervilles*", *Novel*, 18, 1984

—. *The Acoustic Mirror: The Female Voice in Psychoanalysis and Cinema*, Indiana University Press, Bloomington, 1988

A. Simpson, Anne B. "Sue Bridehead Revisited", *Victorian Literature and Culture*, 19, 1991

Anne Smith, ed. *The Novels of Thomas Hardy*, Vision Press, 1979

J. Smith & C. Ferstman. *The Castration of Oedipus: Feminism, Psychopanalysis and the Will to Power*, New York University Press, 1996

J. Sommers. "Hardy's other *Bildungsroman: Tess*", *English Literature in Transition*, 25, 1982

David Sonstroem. "Order and Disorder in *Jude the Obscure*", *English Literature in Transition*, 24, 1981

F.R. Southerington. *Hardy's Vision of Man*, Chatto & Windus, 1971

Dale Spender. *The Writing or the Sex? Why you don't have to read women's writing to know it's no good*, Pergamon Press, New York, NY, 1989

Marlene Springer. *Hardy's Use of Allusion*, Macmillan, London, 1983

R.W. Stallamn. "Hardy's Hour-Glass Novel", *Sewanee Review*, 55, 1947

H. Stevens & C. Howlett, eds. *Modernist Sexualities*, Manchester University Press, 2000

Patricia Stubbs. *Women and Fiction: Feminism and the Novel, 1880-1920*, Harvester, 1979

Rosemary Sumner. *Thomas Hardy: Psychological Novelist*, Macmillan, London, 1981

T. Tanner. "Colour and Movement in Hardy's *Tess of the d'Urbervilles*", *Critical Quarterly*, 10, 1968

Dennis Taylor. *Hardy's Poetry, 1860-1928*, Macmillan, London, 1981

—. "The Second Hardy", *Sewanee Review*, 96, 1988

—. *Hardy's Metres and Victorian Prosody*, Oxford, 1988

Richard H. Taylor. *The Neglected Hardy*, Macmillan, London, 1982

J. Thomas. *Thomas Hardy, Femininity and Dissent*, Palgrave Macmillan, London, 1998

Charlotte Thompson. "Language and the Shape of Reality in *Tess of the d'Urbervilles*", *English Literary History*, 50, 4, 1983

S. Trezise. "Places in Time: Discovering the Chronotope in *Tess of the D'Urbervilles*", *Critical Survey*, 5:2, 1993

Eric Tridgill. *Madonnas and Magdalens: The Origins and Development of Victorian Sexual Attitudes*, Heinemann, 1976

P. Turner. *The Life of Thomas Hardy*, Blackwell, Oxford, 2001

G. Veidemanis. "*Tess of the D'Urbervilles*: What the Film Left Out", *English Journal*, 77:7, 1988

Christopher Walbank. *Thomas Hardy*, Blackie, Glasgow, 1979

C.C. Walcutt. "Character and Coincidence in *The Return of the Native*", in C. Shapiro, 1960

Nell K. Waldman. ""All that she is": Hardy's Tess and Polanski's", *Queen's Quarterly*, 88, 3, 1981

U. Walters. *The Poetry of Thomas Hardy's Novels*, Edwin Mellen Press, 1980

Marina Warner. *Alone Of All Her Sex: The Myth and Cult of the Virgin Mary*, Picador 1985

C. Watts. "Hardy's Sue Bridehead and the 'New Woman'", *Critical*

Survey, 5:2, 1993

Valerie Wayne, ed. *The Matter of Difference: Materialist Feminist Criticism of Shakespeare*, Harvester Wheatsheaf, 1991

Harvey Webster. *On a Darkling Plain*, University of California Press, 1947

R. Webster. "Reproducing Hardy: Familiar and Unfamiliar Versions of *Far from the Madding Crowd* and *Tess of the D'Urbervilles*", *Critical Survey*, 5:2, 1993

Judith Weissman. "The Deceased Wife's Sister Marriage Act and the Ending of *Tess of the d'Urbervilles*", *American Notes and Queries*, 14, 1976

Ottis Wheeler. "Four Versions of *The Return of the Native*", *Nineteenth Century Fiction*, 14, 1959

R.J. White. *Thomas Hardy and History*, Macmillan, London, 1974

Margaret Whitford. *Luce Irigaray: Philosophy in the Feminine*, Routledge, 1991

G. Glen Wickens. "Victorian Theories of Language and *Tess of the d'Urbervilles*", *Mosaic*, 19, 1986

Peter Widdowson. *Hardy in History: A study in literary sociology*, Routledge, 1989

—. *D.H. Lawrence*, Longman, 1992

—. ed. *Thomas Hardy: Tess of the d'Urbervilles: New Casebooks*, Macmillan, London, 1993

—. ed. *Thomas Hardy*, Palgrave Macmillan, London, 1996

Jonathan Wike. "The World as Text in Hardy's Fiction", *Nineteenth Century Literature*, 47, 1993

Linda Ruth Williams. *Critical Desire: Psychoanalysis and the Literary Subject*, Arnold, 1995

—. *Sex in the Head*, Harvester Wheatsheaf, 1995

—. *D.H. Lawrence, Writers and Their Works*, Northcote House, 1997

Merryn Williams. *Thomas Hardy and Rural England*, Macmillan, London, 1972

—. *A Preface to Hardy*, Longman, 1976

K. Wilson. *Thomas Hardy on Stage*, Palgrave Macmillan, London, 1994

George Wing. *Hardy*, Oliver & Boyd, 1963

—. "Theme and Fancy in Hardy's *The Well-Beloved*", *Dalhouse Review*, 56, 1977

Judith Wittenberg. "Angels of Vision and Questions of Gender in *Far From the Madding Crowd*", *The Centennial Review*, 31, 1, 1968

—. "Thomas Hardy's First Novel: Women and the Quest for Autonomy", *Colby Library Quarterly*, 18, 1982

—. "Early Hardy Novels and the Fictional Eye", *Novel*, 16, 1983

Monique Wittig. *The Lesbian Body*, tr. David Le Vay, Beacon Press, Boston 1986

—. *The Straight Mind*, Beacon Press, Boston, 1992

J. Wolmark, ed. *Cybersexualities: A Reader on Feminist Theory, Cyborgs and*

Cyberspace, Edinburgh University Press, 1999

T. Woods. *Beginning Postmodernism,* Manchester University Press, Manchester, 1999

George Wootton. *Thomas Hardy: Towards a Materialist Criticism,* Barnes & Noble, Goldenbridge, 1985

E. Wright, ed. *Feminism and Psychoanalysis: A Critical Dictionary,* Blackwell, 1992

S. Wright. *Thomas Hardy A to Z,* Facts on File Inc, 2002

Terence Wright. *Tess of the d'Urbervilles,* Macmillan, London, 1987

—. *Hardy and the Erotic,* Macmillan, London, 1989

—. "Space, Time, and Paradox: The Sense of History in Hardy's Last Novels", in A. Easson, ed. *History and the Novel, Essays and Studies,* 44, Brewer, Cambridge, 1991

P. Zietlow. *Moments of Vision: The Poetry of Thomas Hardy,* Cambridge, MA, 1974

Jack Zipes. *Don't Bet on the Prince: Contemporary Feminist Fairy Tales in North America and England,* Methuen, New York, NY, 1986

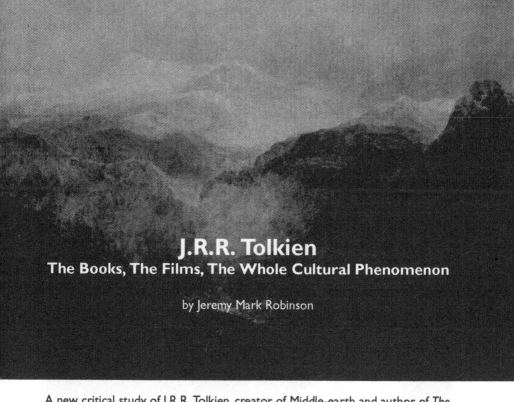

J.R.R. Tolkien
The Books, The Films, The Whole Cultural Phenomenon

by Jeremy Mark Robinson

A new critical study of J.R.R. Tolkien, creator of Middle-earth and author of *The Lord of the Rings*, *The Hobbit* and *The Silmarillion*, among other books.
This new critical study explores Tolkien's major writings (*The Lord of the Rings*, *The Hobbit*, *Beowulf: The Monster and the Critics*, *The Letters*, *The Silmarillion* and *The History of Middle-earth* volumes); Tolkien and fairy tales; the mythological, political and religious aspects of Tolkien's Middle-earth; the critics' response to Tolkien's fiction over the decades; the Tolkien industry (merchandizing, toys, role-playing games, posters, Tolkien societies, conferences and the like); Tolkien in visual and fantasy art; the cultural aspects of The Lord of the Rings (from the 1950s to the present); Tolkien's fiction's relationship with other fantasy fiction, such as C.S. Lewis and *Harry Potter*; and the TV, radio and film versions of Tolkien's books, including the 2001-03 Hollywood interpretations of *The Lord of the Rings*.
This new book draws on contemporary cultural theory and analysis and offers a sympathetic and illuminating (and sceptical) account of the Tolkien phenomenon. This book is designed to appeal to the general reader (and viewer) of Tolkien: it is written in a clear, jargon-free and easily-accessible style.

754pp ISBN 1-86171-057-7 £25.00 / $37.50

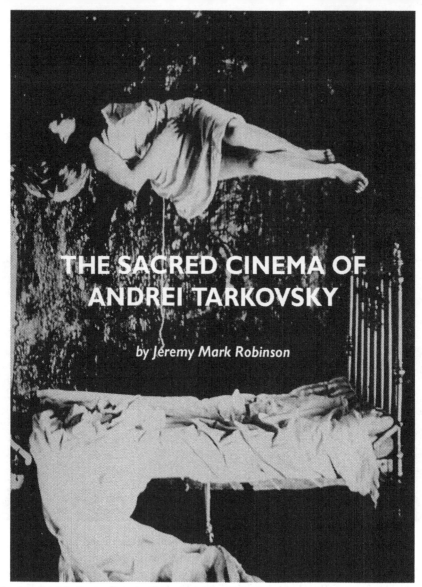

THE SACRED CINEMA OF ANDREI TARKOVSKY

by Jeremy Mark Robinson

A new study of the Russian filmmaker Andrei Tarkovsky (1932-1986), director of seven feature films, including *Andrei Roublyov, Mirror, Solaris, Stalker* and *The Sacrifice*.
This is one of the most comprehensive and detailed studies of Tarkovsky's cinema available. Every film is explored in depth, with scene-by-scene analyses. All aspects of Tarkovsky's output are critiqued, including editing, camera, staging, script, budget, collaborations, production, sound, music, performance and spirituality. Tarkovsky is placed with a European New Wave tradition of filmmaking, alongside directors like Ingmar Bergman, Carl Theodor Dreyer, Pier Paolo Pasolini and Robert Bresson.
An essential addition to film studies.

Illustrations: 150 b/w, 4 colour. 682 pages. First edition. Hardback.

Publisher: Crescent Moon Publishing. Distributor: Gardners Books.

ISBN 1-86171-096-8 (9781861710963) £60.00 / $105.00

The Best of Peter Redgrove's Poetry
The Book of Wonders

by Peter Redgrove, edited and introduced by Jeremy Robinson

Poems of wet shirts and 'wonder-awakening dresses'; honey, wasps and bees; orchards and apples; rivers, seas and tides; storms, rain, weather and clouds; waterworks; labyrinths; amazing perfumes; the Cornish landscape (Penzance, Perranporth, Falmouth, Boscastle, the Lizard and Scilly Isles); the sixth sense and 'extra-sensuous perception'; witchcraft; alchemical vessels and laboratories; yoga; menstruation; mines, minerals and stones; sand dunes; mudbaths; mythology; dreaming; vulvas; and lots of sex magic. This book gathers together poetry (and prose) from every stage of Redgrove's career, and every book. It includes pieces that have only appeared in small presses and magazines, and in uncollected form.

'Peter Redgrove is really an extraordinary poet' (George Szirtes, *Quarto* magazine)
'Peter Redgrove is one of the few significant poets now writing... His 'means' are indeed brilliant and delightful. Technically he is a poet essentially of brilliant and unexpected images...he never disappoints' (Kathleen Raine, *Temenos* magazine).

240pp   ISBN 1-86171-063-1   2nd edition   £19.99 / $29.50

Sex–Magic–Poetry–Cornwall
A Flood of Poems

by Peter Redgrove. Edited with an essay by Jeremy Robinson

A marvellous collection of poems by one of Britain's best but underrated poets, Peter Redgrove. This book brings together some of Redgrove's wildest and most passionate works, creating a 'flood' of poetry. Philip Hobsbaum called Redgrove 'the great poet of our time', while Angela Carter said: 'Redgrove's language can light up a page.' Redgrove ranks alongside Ted Hughes and Sylvia Plath. He is in every way a 'major poet'. Robinson's essay analyzes all of Redgrove's poetic work, including his use of sex magic, natural science, menstruation, psychology, myth, alchemy and feminism.
A new edition, including a new introduction, new preface and new bibliography.

'Robinson's enthusiasm is winning, and his perceptive readings are supported by a very useful bibliography' (*Acumen* magazine)
'*Sex-Magic-Poetry-Cornwall* is a very rich essay... It is like a brightly-lighted box. (Peter Redgrove)
'This is an excellent selection of poetry and an extensive essay on the themes and theories of this unusual poet by Jeremy Robinson' (*Chapman* magazine)

220pp   New, 3rd edition   ISBN 1-86171-070-4   £14.99 / $23.50

THE ART OF ANDY GOLDSWORTHY

COMPLETE WORKS: SPECIAL EDITION
(PAPERBACK and HARDBACK)

by William Malpas

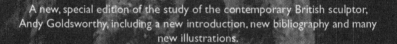

A new, special edition of the study of the contemporary British sculptor, Andy Goldsworthy, including a new introduction, new bibliography and many new illustrations.

This is the most comprehensive, up-to-date, well-researched and in-depth account of Goldsworthy's art available anywhere.

Andy Goldsworthy makes land art. His sculpture is a sensitive, intuitive response to nature, light, time, growth, the seasons and the earth. Goldsworthy's environmental art is becoming ever more popular: 1993's art book *Stone* was a bestseller; the press raved about Goldsworthy taking over a number of London West End art galleries in 1994; during 1995 Goldsworthy designed a set of Royal Mail stamps and had a show at the British Museum. Malpas surveys all of Goldsworthy's art, and analyzes his relation with other land artists such as Robert Smithson, Walter de Maria, Richard Long and David Nash, and his place in the contemporary British art scene.

The Art of Andy Goldsworthy discusses all of Goldsworthy's important and recent exhibitions and books, including the *Sheepfolds* project; the TV documentaries; *Wood* (1996); the New York Holocaust memorial (2003); and Goldsworthy's collaboration on a dance performance.

Illustrations: 70 b/w, 1 colour. 330 pages. New, special, 2nd edition. Publisher: Crescent Moon Publishing. Distributor: Gardners Books.

ISBN 1-86171-059-3 (9781861710598) (Paperback) £25.00 / $44.00

ISBN 1-86171-080-1 (9781861710802) (Hardback) £60.00 / $105.00

CRESCENT MOON PUBLISHING

ARTS, PAINTING, SCULPTURE

The Art of Andy Goldsworthy: Complete Works(Pbk)
The Art of Andy Goldsworthy: Complete Works (Hbk)
Andy Goldsworthy in Close-Up (Pbk)
Andy Goldsworthy in Close-Up (Hbk)
Land Art: A Complete Guide

Richard Long: The Art of Walking
The Art of Richard Long: Complete Works (Pbk)
The Art of Richard Long: Complete Works (Hbk)
Richard Long in Close-Up
Land Art In the UK

Land Art in Close-Up
Installation Art in Close-Up
Minimal Art and Artists In the 1960s and After
Colourfield Painting
Land Art DVD, TV documentary
Andy Goldsworthy DVD, TV documentary
The Erotic Object: Sexuality in Sculpture From Prehistory to the Present Day
Sex in Art: Pornography and Pleasure in Painting and Sculpture
Postwar Art
Sacred Gardens: The Garden in Myth, Religion and Art
Glorification: Religious Abstraction in Renaissance and 20th Century Art
Early Netherlandish Painting
Leonardo da Vinci
Piero della Francesca

Giovanni Bellini
Fra Angelico: Art and Religion in the Renaissance
Mark Rothko: The Art of Transcendence

Frank Stella: American Abstract Artist
Jasper Johns: Painting By Numbers
Brice Marden

Alison Wilding: The Embrace of Sculpture
Vincent van Gogh: Visionary Landscapes
Eric Gill: Nuptials of God
Constantin Brancusi: Sculpting the Essence of Things
Max Beckmann
Egon Schiele: Sex and Death In Purple Stockings
Delizioso Fotografico Fervore: Works In Process 1

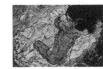

Sacro Cuore: Works In Process 2
The Light Eternal: J.M.W. Turner
The Madonna Glorified: Karen Arthurs

LITERATURE

J.R.R. Tolkien: The Books, The Films, The Whole Cultural Phenomenon
Harry Potter
Sexing Hardy: Thomas Hardy and Feminism
Thomas Hardy's *Tess of the d'Urbervilles*
Thomas Hardy's *Jude the Obscure*
Thomas Hardy: The Tragic Novels
Love and Tragedy: Thomas Hardy
The Poetry of Landscape in Hardy
Wessex Revisited: Thomas Hardy and John Cowper Powys
Wolfgang Iser: Essays
Petrarch, Dante and the Troubadours
Maurice Sendak and the Art of Children's Book Illustration
Andrea Dworkin
Cixous, Irigaray, Kristeva: The *Jouissance* of French Feminism
Julia Kristeva: Art, Love, Melancholy, Philosophy, Semiotics and Psychoanalysis
Hélène Cixous I Love You: The *Jouissance* of Writing
Luce Irigaray: Lips, Kissing, and the Politics of Sexual Difference
Peter Redgrove: Here Comes the Flood
Peter Redgrove: Sex-Magic-Poetry-Cornwall
Lawrence Durrell: Between Love and Death, East and West
Love, Culture & Poetry: Lawrence Durrell
Cavafy: Anatomy of a Soul
German Romantic Poetry: Goethe, Novalis, Heine, Hölderlin, Schlegel, Schiller
Feminism and Shakespeare
Shakespeare: Selected Sonnets
Shakespeare: Love, Poetry & Magic
The Passion of D.H. Lawrence
D.H. Lawrence: Symbolic Landscapes
D.H. Lawrence: Infinite Sensual Violence
Rimbaud: Arthur Rimbaud and the Magic of Poetry
The Ecstasies of John Cowper Powys
Sensualism and Mythology: The Wessex Novels of John Cowper Powys
Amorous Life: John Cowper Powys and the Manifestation of Affectivity (H.W. Fawkner)
Postmodern Powys: New Essays on John Cowper Powys (Joe Boulter)
Rethinking Powys: Critical Essays on John Cowper Powys
Paul Bowles & Bernardo Bertolucci
Rainer Maria Rilke
In the Dim Void: Samuel Beckett
Samuel Beckett Goes into the Silence
André Gide: Fiction and Fervour
Jackie Collins and the Blockbuster Novel
Blinded By Her Light: The Love-Poetry of Robert Graves
The Passion of Colours: Travels In Mediterranean Lands
Poetic Forms
The Dolphin-Boy

POETRY

The Best of Peter Redgrove's Poetry
Peter Redgrove: Here Comes The Flood
Peter Redgrove: Sex-Magic-Poetry-Cornwall
Ursula Le Guin: Walking In Cornwall
Dante: Selections From the Vita Nuova
Petrarch, Dante and the Troubadours
William Shakespeare: Selected Sonnets
Blinded By Her Light: The Love-Poetry of Robert Graves
Emily Dickinson: Selected Poems
Emily Brontë: Poems
Thomas Hardy: Selected Poems
Percy Bysshe Shelley: Poems
John Keats: Selected Poems
D.H. Lawrence: Selected Poems
Edmund Spenser: Poems
John Donne: Poems
Henry Vaughan: Poems
Sir Thomas Wyatt: Poems
Robert Herrick: Selected Poems
Rilke: Space, Essence and Angels in the Poetry of Rainer Maria Rilke
Rainer Maria Rilke: Selected Poems
Friedrich Hölderlin: Selected Poems
Arseny Tarkovsky: Selected Poems
Arthur Rimbaud: Selected Poems
Arthur Rimbaud: A Season in Hell
Arthur Rimbaud and the Magic of Poetry
D.J. Enright: By-Blows
Jeremy Reed: Brigitte's Blue Heart
Jeremy Reed: Claudia Schiffer's Red Shoes
Gorgeous Little Orpheus
Radiance: New Poems
Crescent Moon Book of Nature Poetry
Crescent Moon Book of Love Poetry
Crescent Moon Book of Mystical Poetry
Crescent Moon Book of Elizabethan Love Poetry
Crescent Moon Book of Metaphysical Poetry
Crescent Moon Book of Romantic Poetry
Pagan America: New American Poetry

MEDIA, CINEMA, FEMINISM and CULTURAL STUDIES

J.R.R. Tolkien: The Books, The Films, The Whole Cultural Phenomenon
Harry Potter
Cixous, Irigaray, Kristeva: The *Jouissance* of French Feminism
Julia Kristeva: Art, Love, Melancholy, Philosophy, Semiotics and   Psychoanalysis
Luce Irigaray: Lips, Kissing, and the Politics of Sexual Difference
Hélene Cixous I Love You: The *Jouissance* of Writing
Andrea Dworkin
'Cosmo Woman': The World of Women's Magazines
Women in Pop Music
Discovering the Goddess (Geoffrey Ashe)
The Poetry of Cinema
The Sacred Cinema of Andrei Tarkovsky (Pbk and Hbk)
Paul Bowles & Bernardo Bertolucci
Media Hell: Radio, TV and the Press
An Open Letter to the BBC
Detonation Britain: Nuclear War in the UK
Feminism and Shakespeare
Wild Zones: Pornography, Art and Feminism
Sex in Art: Pornography and Pleasure in Painting and Sculpture
Sexing Hardy: Thomas Hardy and Feminism

In my view *The Light Eternal* is among the very best of all the material I read on Turner. (Douglas Graham, director of the Turner Museum, Denver, Colorado)

The Light Eternal is a model monograph, an exemplary job. The subject matter of the book is beautifully organised and dead on beam. (Lawrence Durrell)

It is amazing for me to see my work treated with such passion and respect. (Andrea Dworkin)

Sex-Magic-Poetry-Cornwall is a very rich essay... It is like a brightly-lighted box. (Peter Redgrove)

CRESCENT MOON PUBLISHING
P.O. Box 393, Maidstone, Kent, ME14 5XU, United Kingdom.
01622-729593 (UK) 01144-1622-729593 (US) 0044-1622-729593 (other territories)
cresmopub@yahoo.co.uk   www.crescentmoon.org.uk

Lightning Source UK Ltd.
Milton Keynes UK
UKOW06f0749080515

251135UK00006B/82/P